Numbers
Games

D1557015

Studies in the
Postmodern Theory of Education

Joe L. Kincheloe and Shirley R. Steinberg
General Editors

Vol. 258

PETER LANG
New York • Washington, D.C./Baltimore • Bern
Frankfurt am Main • Berlin • Brussels • Vienna • Oxford

P. L. Thomas

Numbers Games

Measuring and Mandating American Education

PETER LANG
New York • Washington, D.C./Baltimore • Bern
Frankfurt am Main • Berlin • Brussels • Vienna • Oxford

Library of Congress Cataloging-in-Publication Data

Thomas, P. L. (Paul Lee).
Numbers games: measuring and mandating
American education / P. L. Thomas.
p. cm. — (Counterpoints; v. 258)
Includes bibliographical references and index.
1. Educational tests and measurements—Social aspects—United States.
2. Education and state—United States. I. Title.
II. Series: Counterpoints (New York, N.Y.); v. 258.
LB3051.T46   371.26'0973—dc22   2003027180
ISBN 0-8204-6825-8
ISSN 1058-1634

Bibliographic information published by **Die Deutsche Bibliothek**.
Die Deutsche Bibliothek lists this publication in the "Deutsche
Nationalbibliografie"; detailed bibliographic data is available
on the Internet at http://dnb.ddb.de/.

Cover design by Lisa Barfield

The paper in this book meets the guidelines for permanence and durability
of the Committee on Production Guidelines for Book Longevity
of the Council of Library Resources.

© 2004 Peter Lang Publishing, Inc., New York
275 Seventh Avenue, 28th Floor, New York, NY 10001
www.peterlangusa.com

Printed in the United States of America

To Jessica

CONTENTS

○○○

Introduction
Behind the Numbers—The Uses They Are Put To 1

Part I
Numbers Games, American Style

Chapter 1
The American Psyche, Measured and Certain 11
    Scientific Methods, American Style.....................................13
    Numbers, Numbers—All There in Black and White 18
    Abracadabra—The Magical Power of Numbers............................24
    "It's the Economy, Stupid"—Numbers and Money in America......27
    Majorities Rule, Don't They? 32
    We're Number 1!...33
    If Numbers Predict, Then Why Play the Game?.........................35
    A Tale of Three Truths—Poetic, Historical, and Statistical..............37
    Counting on the American Psyche.......................................40

Chapter 2
Politics, Media, and Education—
Honesty among the Numbers 43
    Of Research and Data—The Politics of Loving Numbers.................45
    A New Honesty in Education—
    Positivist Measures in a Postmodern World 49
    Political Agendas and Public Schools—It Came from the 1980s 67
    Profits and Prophets of Doom—
    Textbooks and Reading Programs.......................................70

Blind-sided from the Right—
Print Media, Science, Numbers, and Schools 73
Talking Numbers—Approaching the Truth....................................75

Part II
Numbers Games in the Classroom and against the Classroom

Chapter 3
The Numbers and Forces behind Teaching Practices 81
Covering Content and Planning for the Future 82
Reseeing the Classroom—
Quantifying (and Confusing) Means and Ends 83
The Weight of Numbers in the Classroom....................................90
Should Teachers Bow to Tests? No..92
Counting on Assumptions of Classroom Teachers 103
    The Bell-Shaped Curve Rings Loudly....................................104
    Just Add the Grades and Do the Average, Dummy!..................106
    He's a "C" Student, and She's a Solid "A-" 108
    It's Rank to Be Ranked 109
    Giving Them What They Want—Reporting Grades.................110
    The Dangers of Quantifying—Fearing the Rubric.................112
    The Reasons for Grading 113
    Does Any Question Really Matter? 114
    The Onus of Being Labeled Smart—Or Not 114
    Starting from Nothing—Of Zero and One Hundred..............116
    Objecting to the Behavioral Objective—
    It Must Be Measurable 117

Chapter 4
Dismantling Public Education by the Numbers 119
The Politics of How We Teach—
NCLB as Assault on Academia 121
Numbers as Smoke and Mirrors—
NCLB as Flawed Mandate 131
It's Not So Simple—Addressing Literacy and Poverty 135
    Well-Intentioned Misconceptions...136
    Making the Connection...139
Discrediting Schools by the Numbers—
Why Vouchers and Choice Fail..142

Conclusion
Beyond the Numbers to the Students We Teach..........................155

References 159

✥ INTRODUCTION

○○○

Behind the Numbers—
The Uses They Are Put To

It was written in the 1950s, and it's fiction, I admit. But within the world created by Kurt Vonnegut (1980) in *Player Piano*, eerie parallels exist with the modern political wrestling match we call American public education. One exchange captures ideas important to us here: The main character, Paul, questions another character, Lasher, about the harsh treatment of manager and engineers compared to the apparent ignoring of the scientists; Lasher points out that scientists only give society knowledge so they cannot be held accountable for the way we apply that knowledge. As with much of Vonnegut's work, in the world of *Player Piano*, a great deal of scientific knowledge is being applied in the worst possible ways.

In Vonnegut's world, most workers have been replaced by machines, the worth of every human determined by IQ tests that label each person for life, the data stored in a centralized personnel system that regulates what people can and cannot do for their jobs. Tests scores are graphed, and everything revolves around economic efficiency: If machines save money over human workers, then machines it is!

And therein lies the crux of all we will explore in the following pages concerning the complex and troubling world of American public education as it intersects science that quantifies, the business paradigm, and the grand manipulations of politicians (and how this drama plays out in the media). All of this, of course, swirls around and through the average person in our democratic society—the populace who themselves are as disserved by the process as the students who walk the halls of our schools.

• • •

Over the hundred-year span of American public education, numbers assumptions have negatively impacted the daily job of being a teacher and adversely affected student learning. Politicians, educrats, and journalists have fed those numbers assumptions in the American psyche a steady diet of oversimplified and distorted data that read as if fact. In other words, the typical American *believes* wholeheartedly that a student's SAT score means something that it doesn't (or at least more than it does) and unflinchingly accepts that average SAT scores for a state clearly reflect the quality of all education in that state.

This book will trace four basic areas of the numbers games played with our schools and our students—the numbers assumptions and lay perceptions about science and research in the general American psyche; the numbers manipulations by politicians and the media (including self-appointed pundits who consider themselves experts on education); the general and institutionalized numbers-based classroom practices by teachers that need reconsideration and even abandonment; and the most recent assault on literacy education by the federal government through the manipulation of quantitative data (in the form of George W. Bush's education legislation popularly known as No Child Left Behind), along with a vigorous call for privatizing schools.

The big ideas of this book, the ideas that weave their way through each chapter, target *with skepticism* system assumptions that behave like Truths and paradigms when that system doesn't acknowledge or allow reflection or dialogue. Both the bureaucracy of government and the public school system have suffered from a conservative and reductionistic nature that often ignores or even dehumanizes the personal elements of a democracy, of educating people, and of interpreting research and then implementing practices based on those conclusions.

One big idea revolves around the debate between quantitative and qualitative research and data. Primarily, I look at the dominance of quantitative data in America (fueled by our commitment to capitalism along with one narrow and distorted perception of what constitutes being "scientific"), while also showing the contribution qualitative research offers in a valid and authentic way for democracy and education. The strengths and weaknesses of both paradigms are explored, though there is an advocacy for qualitative research included in the following pages (but no intent to discount the potential value of quantitative data).

This discussion also traces in broad fashion the implicit American choice of *quantifying* as the crux of science over the *scientific method* as the heart of science. From the IQ to SAT to state assessment data, Americans are likely to believe as fact the simplified information provided by numbers; we trust averages and believe in the bell-shaped curve, the scientific ability to predict the distribution of all phenomena. As a counterbalance, I show that most of the leading progressive educators of the first half of the 20th century meant for education to embrace the organic and open-ended nature of the scientific method as the guiding force for improving both our educational system and ultimately our democracy.

While those big ideas pervade the American culture, I also deal with a few big ideas entrenched in the public education system. Within our classrooms—from teacher education to teacher induction to continuing teacher assessment—behavioristic learning theory, analytic instruction and learning, quantitative assessment, and linear thinking are inculcated in teachers as if these assumptions are without debate or alternatives, chiseled in stone tablets. That systematic norm reinforces both within education and throughout the larger community the oversimplifications that inhibit more effective education from being fulfilled. These educational assumptions contribute greatly to the numbers games within schools that in turn feed the numbers games played by politicians and journalists with the average American.

A final big idea at the heart of American public education (of universal education as an act of human emancipation) involves the great mistakes we have made in literacy education. Schools function as if all learning must be approached analytically by breaking holistic endeavors into their smallest component parts. Driven by the behaviorism engine, we assume that everything is easier in small chunks:

> By reducing each human action to its smallest unit, that of stimulus and response, Thorndike and later John B. Watson (Watson, et al., 1917), another major behaviorist, sought to establish the principles of human behavior that would permit its prediction. (Pinar, Reynolds, Slattery, & Taubman, 1996, p. 92)

The numbers games and the concurrent analytic assumptions have combined to do more harm than good to learners of reading and writing. In fact, most children would be better served learning literacy skills naturally than to have reading reduced to phonics and writing reduced to grammar, both drilled daily through mind-numbing worksheets in isolation. That analytic approaches to literacy are more instructionally manageable, more easily tested, and more readily quantified has allowed best practice for reading and writing instruction to be essentially ignored on a large scale throughout the last 100 years.

I am moved to write this book as an advocate for literacy education as *the* most important avenue to personal empowerment and voice needed within a democracy, as an advocate for practicing teachers who have had their field deprofessionalized systematically throughout the 20th century (Lofty, 2003), and as an advocate for qualitative researchers who deserve at least equal access to the scholarly debates at the heart of a healthy and vibrant educational system.

For nearly 20 years I have been a literacy educator and a writer. For more than half of that career, I have also become a qualitative researcher who believes action research, biography, case studies, and the like are closer to being authentic data for the human endeavor of educating than stanine scores on a norm-referenced test or an SAT score for college scholarships. But during my teaching career I have seen the cyclic nature of time tilt most often to numbers games at the expense of children and teachers, at the expense of their humanity and their abilities to participate fully in a democracy.

• • •

For this discussion and to enhance the readability of the following chapters, I need to clarify here the major terms and concepts as I will be using them. Education, public education, is necessarily of interest to all within a democracy—from the daily discussions on the street to the esoteric musings of intellectuals within the halls of universities who call public education their field. This book is intended for general and professional audiences, so I will attempt to wrestle with ideas big and small for the benefit of all readers.

At the core of this discussion, and how education functions, are the terms *positivism* and *quantitative research*—both of which function under a clear set of assumptions:

1) in the same circumstances many people will have the same experiences; 2) the majority dictates reality; 3) the individual is omitted in understanding a

situation, i.e., generalization rather than what is unique is important; 4) there is a tendency to treat subjects as means to an end; 5) quantitative research pretends that objectivity, including political neutrality, is possible by eradicating subjectivity and ideology. (Pinar, Reynolds, Slattery, & Taubman, 1996, p. 53)

Throughout the discussion, I hope to consider the limitations of both positivistic and quantitative assumptions, their potential value also being encouraged.

Quantitative research strives to measure and label phenomenon with numbers—lending itself to averages, ranges, rankings, generalizability, etc. Often portrayed as a softer approach in the natural sciences, *qualitative research* embraces a research methodology that explores small populations (as small as one person in biography) and aims to describe phenomenon in its complexity, unearthing questions more often than building conclusions; for the qualitative researcher, the unique, the outlier is of more interest than generalizability. Qualitative researchers perform biography, case studies, ethnography, and such. While the quantitative researcher values detached researchers and objectivity, the qualitative researcher is an active participant who more often than not admits bias and the unavoidable distortions of human perception. Broadly, qualitative research offers this: "Part of what we might learn is living with uncertainty" (Silverman, 1993, p. 210). And the quantitative researcher will have none of that.

Difficult to separate from the distinction between quantitative and qualitative research are the ideologies within which they function—*modernism* and *postmodernism*. Broadly explained, modernism supports the assumptions of quantitative research—the possibility of objectivity, the validity of quantifying, and the existence of definable and unwavering Truth. Sprung from the modernist mind-set as a refutation is postmodernism, which encompasses qualitative assumptions (all human perception is subjective, most of existence is beyond quantifying, and truth is elusive and relative) and possibly nonexistent.

As the modernism and postmodernism debate has grown during the past 50 or so years, that tension over perception has impacted most academic fields, science included. *Science* as a broad term will be used throughout this book; a large portion of the discussion will be raising the question, What is science? Further, I will be exploring what *should* science mean or how *might* science best serve public edu-

cation and the American democracy. Since I am acknowledging that
the term has at least a muddled meaning throughout society, I will
save attempting to define "science" for the shifting discussion
throughout the text.

Yet, here I should clarify that my essential concern about the varied and conflicting perceptions of the term "science" revolves around
what I will refer to as *"vulgar scientism"*—the reduced and distorted
view of science as quantifying, the view that science identifies static
truth (Flinders & Thornton, 1997, p. 39)—as it contrasts with "science"
as a field guided by the *scientific method*. The scientific method as an
organic process that both acknowledges and embraces the shifting
nature of reality, the chaotic nature of human existence and perception, stands for me in this discussion as both the most accurate perception of science and the most effective use of science for education.
Within that context, I feel that everyone within the educational community, from researchers and scholars to administrators and practitioners, needs to embrace the latter perception of science if our
schools are to serve students and society well.

The pragmatism of John Dewey (who ironically garners a great
deal of credit and blame for his impact on American education—a
distortion of the greatest kind since Dewey has had virtually no impact on the actual classroom practices of American education during
the past 100 years; in fact, his impact is subsumed entirely by the
dominance of the behavioral psychologists and positivists) offers
educators the best focus for conducting both overarching curricular
decisions and daily classroom practices—*warranted assertions*.
Dewey's science would have practitioners in education base their curricular, instructional, and assessment decisions on the growing body
of evidence, implementing what appears best at that moment (a warranted assertion), while also acknowledging that as the evidence ac-
cumulates, those warranted assertions may, and usually will, change.
And numbers may often be in that mix, but those numbers would be
seen as partial and temporary representations of reality, not conclusions to dictate future events.

Correlation and *causation* add further complications when the
numbers attached to our students and our schools are dumped into
the purview of the general public. Correlation between two phenomena may or may not show some degree of causation, yet more often
than not, the popular assumption of correlation is causation. Gould
(1996) explains: "Noncausal correlations are the bane of statistical in-

ference. . . . They are perfectly 'true' in the mathematical sense, but they demonstrate no causal connection" (p. 151). In other words, sometimes numbers tell us something, a correlation, but do not give us what we want, a causational relationship between phenomena. Yet, the common perception of most data is to assume such causation when a correlation exists.

Let me offer a few brief examples. From the daily newspaper to advertisement spots on VH1, most Americans have heard the great news; classical music (No! Music of any kind!) makes kids smart, so please save our music programs. This "Mozart effect" has become a part of the national consciousness, but the study upon which the causation has been assumed suggests no more than a correlation. The music experiences of children may have some correlation with better reading and math scores in students; the music itself may actually be merely a *marker*, though, for dozens of other stimuli or occurrences that are impacting learning. Like studies that show higher National Merit Scholarships from families that eat together, the Mozart effect is a complex issue of deciphering where there is mere correlation (that two or more events have some sort of relationship, a relationship that very well may not include one event causing the other) and where there is causation (that some event actually causes another). Eating meals with your child while playing Mozart in the background will certainly *not* cause higher student achievement if hundreds of other factors are not in place; and further research may show that the meals together and the music may be of no value when compared to those other factors.

Finally, the last chapter will narrow to the literacy debate since it is so heavily impacted by the numbers games. *Whole language* and *phonics* have suffered a simplistic and horribly distorted debate for nearly 100 years. Phonics instruction, as I will use the phrase here, means directly teaching students the many sound patterns of the alphabet in the English language; that instruction is often isolated, decontextualized from whole and authentic texts and from the students' own speaking or reading. The whole language philosophy, which itself has been greatly misrepresented and improperly practiced for decades, offers a paradigm for teaching students to read based on the following assumptions:

1. Speech is a natural human function more or less pre-wired in the brain.

2. From birth, children need language-rich environments that support their natural ability to acquire language.

3. Every child needs the *least* amount of direct phonics instruction possible to set in motion natural language acquisition. Little or no direct phonics instruction is needed after about first grade when most students are well on their way to developing linguistic skills from being engaged in language activities.

4. Direct phonics instruction should begin with each child (at each child's current level of *demonstrated* phonemic awareness) based on student performances of language (speaking or reading aloud, for instance) and within the context of authentic literature and language-rich activities with advanced language users.

• • •

Two-thirds of the way through Vonnegut's *Player Piano*, the reader learns of scientifically- and machine-driven medical practices: Here, doctors make no decisions on their own; they simply implement the steps machines tell them to do. In Vonnegut's world, numbers and measuring have replaced human expertise. While such a farfetched situation in the novel may seem silly when we consider the work of medical doctors, that same scenario is eerily similar to how we view the work of teachers today—measure the children's learning and dictate what steps teachers take. But teaching, like the practice of healing, is ultimately a human endeavor, more than measuring and more than standardizing instruction.

Numbers are an integral part of the American psyche, as is our institution of public education. For many years these forces have worked against each other. The following pages will make a plea to parents, teachers, administrators, journalists, pundits, and politicians to set aside our agendas—to rethink our suppositions ourselves—and see the children behind the numbers.

 # PART 1

○○○

Numbers Games, American Style

Our religious and cultural heritage is to deny, for all we're worth, that we're in any way connected with the rest of life on earth. We don't come from it, we're not part of it; we *own* it and were put down here to run the place.
—*Barbara Kingsolver*

History demonstrates that people will find ingenious ways and develop elaborate constructs to create and harden categories of status and privilege among groups that constitute humankind. And they will produce a litany of justifications to convince the populace that these inequalities are natural and right.
—*John I. Goodlad*

 # ONE

The American Psyche, Measured and Certain

Americans love numbers. In fact, we are fond of saying, with emphatic confidence, even arrogance, things such as, "Numbers don't lie," whether we are talking about sports, the economy, politics—or our public school system. We love numbers. We *believe* in numbers.

This is no recent phenomenon, but an evolving one over the last 150 years, sprung from the primordial ooze of Charles Darwin and all the other folk who turned America and the world around a corner and into the Modern World—the world of science, electronic gadgetry, microwave ovens, heat-seeking missiles, and the Bomb. The American psyche today is entrenched in a peculiarly quantifying and predictive scientific way of thinking, one that is reinforced and shaped by our other assumptions as a culture. There is a cross-pollination lurking in our modern longing for the scientific, our religious dogmatism, our lingering affection for the mystical, and our commitment to capitalism (actually, big "C" Capitalism) at the expense of democracy.

Our numbers compulsion reinforces a science that quantifies and predicts, that is above all else certain. All systems function with assumptions that serve as paradigms or Truths—yes, the big "T" truths. And for America, when we speak about most everything, especially education, anything that is measurable should be measured, we believe, and, well, numbers don't lie.

• • •

In this postmodern world, when we are supposed to have left naiveté behind, our symbol of being scientific is probably the computer and more recently the icon-driven world of Windows software. And that computer is infallible and powerful (more on that power later), driven as it is by numbers, its own little binary code. If there is any doubt about the American love for numbers, look closely at the computer market, the war between computer companies seeking customers. It's all about numbers. Megahertz and gigabytes, (my monitor is bigger than your monitor), faster Internet connection speeds, and the like.

The simple measure itself identifies for American consumers quality. Americans believe wholeheartedly that quantity equals quality.

• • •

Speaking of consumers, consider our commercials. Advertising is saturated in the U.S. with diet concerns. And how is American health measured? Weight. Maybe your cholesterol number, your blood pressure, or your resting pulse, as well. But we believe that weight represents health, or lack of it.

Yes, we are guided through commercials by numbers. One commercial that stays in my mind advertises a home security company. In the ad, when a house's security alarm is armed, binary code floods the walls of the house, making it safe. There is a subtle metaphor there, to me, about the American psyche, flooded as it is with numbers. Like that armed house flooded with numbers, a sign of strength and safety, such is the American mind.

• • •

There's an episode of "Everybody Loves Raymond" when Raymond actually says, "Numbers don't lie." In this episode, Raymond's brother, Robert, gives Raymond and his wife IQ tests; oddly, the brief scenes showing the administering of the test include fact-based questions—clearly not an IQ test, though that show plays on the average person's perception that intelligence is fact-based.

The show is funny since Robert manipulates his family by changing who has the highest IQ to see how they each behave. But for us, the show captures the writers' understandings of the essence of our perceptions of intelligence as shown through knowledge of facts and our belief in numbers. As Raymond says to his wife when he believes he has the higher IQ, "Numbers don't lie."

• • •

While this is an extremely complicated argument about numbers games in America and how that ultimately impacts our education system—that those with power measure and mandate how we teach and how we assess learning—some things can be clearly delineated about the dangers of quantitative data as it impacts living our lives or the organized education of humans, especially when the numbers are interpreted simplistically by a lay audience, including our politicians. As well, alongside the dangers of the positivist world, the value of the qualitative world becomes more clearly revealed.

Americans love numbers, but the assumptions and conclusions drawn from those numbers cause the greatest problems, and are most ripe for manipulation. Several areas of our numbers games can expose those complexities—defining "scientific," dogmatic thinking, the mystical power of numbers, our capitalistic commitment, our narrowed view of democracy, the conflict between prescriptive and descriptive data, and our quest for Truth, in its many outfits. Let's play with each of these for a while and see the many stories numbers seem to tell.

Scientific Methods, American-Style

Insert here, in your mind, the opening to Stanley Kubrick's movie *2001: A Space Odyssey*. It's a good effect, and it's relevant for a number of reasons, some coming later. The movie opens with "The Dawn of Man" scene and unforgettable music.

Let's go back ourselves to a particular dawn of science, when the world began to creep toward the modern and scientific world, just before one of those magical turns of the century, the 20th. Back to the ooze of Darwin and those like him. Yes, science has older roots, but I see the late 1800s as a pivotal time because of the profound impact of evolutionary theory. That Darwin gave the world the *debate* is key to our discussion of numbers, and our concern for how we live and how we teach.

• • •

Preparing for a course I teach in curriculum, I reread a piece by Herb Kliebard. In the final lines of the excerpt, Kliebard refers to "a simplistic and vulgar scientism" (Flinders & Thornton, 1997, p. 39). So we'll borrow his term, "vulgar scientism," to make a distinction about this peculiarly American fascination with numbers and reductionistic science, as it contrasts with a pure thus accurate perception of "science."

Teaching literature affords numerous opportunities to deal with many topics, and each year when I taught Ernest Hemingway's *The Sun Also Rises*, we paused at a scene that alludes to the Scopes trial and the joke—Which came first, the chicken or the egg? Teaching in a conservative Southern town always made the debate surrounding evolution interesting. And revealing.

To provoke that discussion, I suggested to my students that the chicken/egg gag is not just something they have heard on "Sesame Street," not just all fun and games. I told them that the answer suggests where someone stands in the evolution/creationism debate. If you answer "chicken," you are a creationist, believing the chicken sprang full blown from the mind of God; if you answer "egg," then you are an evolutionist, embracing the possibility that creatures come from something before them on this planet. Then we would argue.

One hundred and fifty years after Darwin, we all still argue about evolution and how to teach it. That debate usually reveals the American conception of "scientific." For my students, and for the average person on the street, science is about fact and truth and numbers and certainty—*vulgar scientism*. And for many, ironically, that narrow conception of science merges with their dogmatic religious faith, grounded strongly in the mystical and those things outside of the empirical realm. If evolution is a quantifiable fact, an empirical truth, they seem to think, then it discounts other Truth that is not quantifiable, their creationism (Raymo, 1998). We'll come to this again.

• • •

For Charles Darwin and all scientists, the concept of "scientific" is profoundly different from the vulgar scientism of the American psyche, the urge to quantify and document as permanent fact. At its core, science grows from the scientific method—hypothesize, experiment, draw tentative conclusions, and then do it all again within the community of equally educated and informed peers. Scientists live in a world of temporal conclusions, expecting new evidence to reveal itself, expecting the conclusions to change and to be refined, sharpened to the finest point imaginable. The modern pragmatic movement in philosophy and education, personified by John Dewey, challenged America to choose this path of warranted assertion, but that avenue proved too complex; tentative knowing somehow does not fulfill a basic human need to be certain.

The science we could have chosen is expressed well by Gould (1996) in his argument about IQ and the open-ended nature of knowing in science:

> Working scientists are generally good at analyzing data. We are trained to spot fallacies of argument and, especially, to be hypercritical of supporting data. We scrutinize charts and look at every dot on a graph. Science moves forward as much by critiquing the conclusion of others as by making novel discoveries. (p. 25)

Pure science, then, science that springs from the organic nature of the scientific method, is itself in a state of evolution. Take for example how the medical profession works, especially in comparison to education, which I'll deal with directly toward the end of this discussion.

Antibiotics have traveled an interesting and shifting path in the modern world based on new and changing empirical data. At first, when we stumbled onto the power of antibiotics, their effect seemed miraculous. Through the scientific method, scientists and the public eventually got it—how antibiotics work and what antibiotics can work to cure. Over decades, though, the public *belief* in antibiotics overpowered the science of the medical profession; the result was a panic over the negative effects of overprescribing antibiotics, drug-resistant infections. When the empirical data revealed the health risks of unnecessarily prescribed antibiotics, medical practitioners changed their practices, despite public outcry.

The lesson is: Beware the power of the popular misunderstanding of science. In medicine, as the case needs to be with education, the more sophisticated and complex understandings of the professional practitioners must outweigh the often simplistic and misguided understandings of the public at large.

One more brief example and comparison: If a mother of twins were to take her children to a doctor and that doctor found only one of the children to have an infection, would that mother demand that the doctor treat both children the same, prescribing both medication? Certainly not. And even if she did, the doctor surely would not comply. Yet daily in the U.S., parents (and politicians, thus "standards") are demanding that teachers treat all students the same; reading and writing instruction for all fourth graders, for example, are being monitored so that every teacher teaches the same things at the same times and in the same manner. Ridiculous.

• • •

Between Darwin's *The Origin of Species* and the Scopes trial in the 1920s, America also experienced a growth and transition in industry. Taylorism swept factories and eventually invaded schools. Floor managers and principals alike began to measure against the clock, to quantify time-on-task in order to predict and standardize both production (most possible work for the least amount of pay) and education.

This mania in industry helped inspire Upton Sinclair's *The Jungle*, and some in American society began to recognize the dangers of unbridled measurement in the face of the human condition. Yet throughout the 20th century, both industry and education have fallen victim time and again to those dangers, though education has never had its own *The Jungle* (in fact, most of the voices raised concerning education over the years have fueled the problem, not called for any real change). Throughout the modern history of American education, we have seen a strong influence by industry on education. Taylorism contributed positively to profit margins in industry, and it fed the developing American perception of "scientific" being about numbers and measurement, about efficiency as the primary marker of value. To the lay public and politicians, that same vulgar scientism appeared to be the obvious modern approach needed for education; teaching and learning need to be more efficient. Simple.

Then we began to see this kudzu of the mind that would continue to envelope the American psyche until it became the default mind-set of Americans—science is about measuring and finding numbers that prove. What does that mean in our daily lives, in our perceptions?

To most Americans, saying that something is scientific means a variety of things in different arenas. "Scientific" means safe and healthy, it means the information is valuable; but it means above all else that something has been proven, permanently. I should mention: Americans don't just love numbers; we love facts, to be right, damn it!—whether it is the word of God or a handy and simple statistic. And science, sweet science, gives us facts, facts we can use to crush the ignorant, even though we have had to concoct a way to accept a certain type of vulgar scientism while rejecting pure science that often steps on our collective religious toes.

• • •

Indirectly, the American psyche has come to respect numbers and even expect numbers to make things legitimate. We have weather channels with the weather quantified across the bottom of our TV

screens (even windchill and real-feel heat formulas since mere ther-
mometers are not enough) and convenient number systems to quantify the power of tornadoes and hurricanes; we have financial news
networks with the stock market data scrolling across the screen; we
have simple charts and graphs with numbers and percentages on the
fronts of our newspapers, our *colorful* newspapers. And not only do
our children receive grades to represent what they know, what they
have learned, parents now also receive report cards on our schools,
report cards filled with data and charts and graphs, even showing
where all the money goes.

And that's a shame. America had a choice, way back when the
drums were sounding over Darwin's head—bum-bum, bum-bum.
One path led to the pure scientific mind, an organic way of thinking
and living, a paradigm that acknowledges change and growth, and
values the quest instead of the prize at the end of the rainbow; and
this science, the science of Einstein and Dewey, would and can serve
our educational system and our free society well. The other path, vulgar scientism, lured our collective mind onto the road easiest traveled, where this complex world can be measured, quantified,
simplified, and captured, crystallized, caged for all to see. And *that*
science has fathered virtually everything that is wrong with our public schools.

• • •

Numbers pervade the American culture in a way that screams
verification. Four out of five dentists prefer this toothpaste. Pop music
and the movie industry thrive on number of albums sold, box office
receipts, and the number of stars or thumbs-up they can garner. Even
our sacred sports are number-laden. College football is now driven by
a computer formula that determines who plays for the national
championship; college basketball teams are slaves to an index that
rates the power of their schedules—and that formula is their ticket to
March Madness and millions of dollars. Michael Jordan became a
megastar by leading the NBA in scoring; professional football quar-
terbacks now have a number rating to show who is best (even years
ago it was passing yards per season).

America loves its entertainment industry and its sports, and we
have imbued both with our zeal for numbers. And if anyone has the
audacity to criticize the quality of any of those stars, people are quick
to pull out the numbers: look how many people bought that record,
look how much money she has, look how many rings he wears.

And just listen to our youth when we dare to challenge the value of entertainers or athletes. When I was a beginning teacher, even then, I enjoyed teaching by rattling students' cages. One day we talked about a local college's star player signing a huge contract with a successful pro football team. After the player had been interviewed on a local news channel, I pointed out that he may have served his college's reputation better if he had tapped his foot once for "yes" and twice for "no" during the interview; I was joking about how we Southerners sound pretty ignorant out loud on TV. But a student took offense and blurted out, "He makes more money than you do," and that justified everything.

Miller (1999) wrestles with the persistent conflict between science and religion in his book *Finding Darwin's God*. He clarifies that "[s]cientific knowledge, in the absolute sense, is always tentative" (p. 21). As well, he argues that the American psyche leans toward the law, not science, in the arguing of ideas: "Lawyers are advocates. Their task is not necessarily to seek the truth, but to present a particular point of view as forcefully and effectively as they can" (p. 122). Miller's discussion helps us understand how Americans can simultaneously embrace science in some forms, such as technology, then boldly deny scientific knowledge, such as evolution, even in the face of *evidence*, the cornerstone of the scientific process.

Yet, it's not that simple. While I do argue that for the American psyche at large, numbers have a certain vulgar scientism to them, much more is at play when we see numbers and embrace them as fact, fact that predicts and judges.

At the heart of America's somewhat blind and distorted view of numbers and what they mean is an ironic need for predicting, standardizing, and legitimizing *America*. Further, I believe, a number of other factors in the American psyche have helped shape that vulgar scientism that is in our daily lives and driving our schools, one of which is, ironically, our dogmatic religiosity.

Numbers, Numbers—
All There in Black and White

While listening to talk radio, I caught the end of a discussion about a wealthy liberal offering to put up the money to begin a leftwing talk-radio slate of shows to compete with the growing success of right-wing talk radio. One of the Smothers Brothers, from TV fame, stated that he felt no liberal would ever be popular, no liberal could appeal to the general public since liberals deal in grays, and conservatives, in black and white.

I think that to be an accurate observation and one that serves us well as we try to understand the reductionistic nature of the American public's dealing with numbers and research, what we call "scientific." Further, we can look into the work of Howard Gardner (1991, 1996) on how we think and what qualities are common in the great leaders throughout history. There we can begin to see some of the broad forces that have shaped and continue to shape what we accept as fact and truth, especially when portrayed through numbers.

Gardner makes two points that I believe are connected, two points that when connected support my argument about America's misuse of numbers and science. Gardner offers a refined and helpful re-explanation of Piaget's description of cognitive development. For Gardner (1991), children first pass through a 5-year-old mind, one that functions in the black/white, right/wrong, good/evil paradigms. This immature or unsophisticated approach to ideas, in fact, was directly attacked by John Dewey and a whole host of progressive educators during the last 100 years. Early in life, children see everything as the flip of a coin, as Raymo (1998) explains about True Believers.

Gardner helps us understand that humans pass through several identifiable stages of cognition, of thinking. What he also shows is that humans *retain* all of those stages (the more sophisticated stage does not subsume the earlier stage; the brain here does *not* act like a computer overwriting a file of the same name on the hard drive) and are at times apt to revert to the most basic patterns of thought, notably the 5-year-old mind. I would argue that when we see the collective mind of any large group of people, the phenomenon of groupthink tends to be in the black-and-white mode of thought. Consider Gardner's work on leaders.

In that work, Gardner (1996) explores the minds of great leaders—Gandhi, Margaret Thatcher, Martin Luther King, Jr., and several others. One recurring conclusion drawn by Gardner is that successful leaders must be exceptional communicators, but that their messages must be *simple*. I believe that Gardner's work suggests that as a collective, societies, cultures, or any organized body functions at the 5-year-old mentality, seeing everything in black-and-white dualities.

When we look closely at how leaders, or even advertisements, appeal to the public en masse, a clear parallel reveals itself between the most basic form of childhood thinking, black-and-white distinctions, and how *groups* think. In popular culture such either/or mentalities have manifested themselves in good guys versus bad guys entertainment. Are the white and black hats of early Westerns so far removed from the American psyche today? The rhetoric of our political leaders both feeds and manipulates that dualistic thinking. As I write this, the U.S. president has declared that people are either with us or against us as we prepare to invade Iraq; the same either/or stance is repeated daily on talk radio concerning war protests. And the appeal appears to work, according to scientific polls. Does not that suggest that as a collective even a sophisticated society such as America thinks as a 5-year-old mind? I believe so.

• • •

I recently read a news article by Steven Pinker, a leading expert on linguistics today, someone I reference and read often in my own work as a literacy educator. In one sentence of his article, he completely discounted whole language instruction. I was flabbergasted.

From experts to the average person, we are all subject to accepting at face value what amounts to nothing more than urban legend. Although credible researchers such as Stephen Krashen and Regie Routman have shown that the failure of whole language *never happened*, the political rhetoric accompanied by a whole array of numbers and statistics have made the failure true in the American mind. We like "this versus that" debates; we also love to choose sides, especially when one side is solid and clear and the other fuzzy.

If you look throughout the history of political, economic, or educational debates in America, a disturbing pattern exists—opposing dualities. The general public, and even academic experts, have fallen into the trap of phonics versus whole language instruction despite such dualities being false arguments to begin with. As with many "this versus that" arguments, no coin flip actually exists. To stay with the reading debate, one cannot simply pick phonics or whole language; the reading debate is actually *how* one addresses reading, not *if* we teach phonemic awareness. Few people know or can even accept that phonemic instruction is a component of whole language theory.

• • •

For most of my 18 years as a public school English teacher, I was lucky. The principal during the largest part of that time was very supportive of me as a writing teacher, openly praising my ability to teach students to write. I have been an advocate of holistic writing instruction throughout my career, rejecting isolated and decontextualized grammar and vocabulary instruction. While that principal was supportive, he also once in a faculty meeting said that in our English department we did not teach grammar.

Why? Despite the overwhelming evidence that holistic writing instruction had served my students quite well for years, he was unconsciously a victim of dualistic thinking: Teachers who have students write must be against grammar; teachers who have students read must be against phonics. The flaw with this thinking is, again, a "not-if"-but-"how" dilemma. (I'll come to this again.)

In that faculty meeting, numbers spurred his misinformed comment. The principal and assistant principal were showing and discussing student performances from the past year on two distinct sets of data—the results of the Advanced Placement (AP) exams from The College Board (all of which require created responses along with selected-response sections) and the norm-referenced, selected-response-only California Test of Basic Skills (CTBS).

The dilemma created by the data concerned what constitutes fair measures of language arts skills, basically reading and writing. While the AP exam in Literature and Composition required students to write original essays based on literary readings, the CTBS test assessed students through multiple-choice questions that isolated reading skills and only assessed students' abilities to edit sentences for grammar and mechanics out of context and not of their own writing.

After the principal stated that we didn't teach grammar, I noted that several of our advanced students who had scored 4s (the next-to-the-highest score) on an AP exam had relatively low CTBS scores on the "writing" section of that test, *though students never actually composed any writing on that exam*. The complicated truth of the data (the conflicting information on language arts scores of our students) was that the CTBS test was flawed, not our teaching, not the student learning, and certainly not because we didn't teach grammar. Again, the discussion about writing instruction continues to be not *if* we teach grammar, but *how* we foster written expression with grammatical dexterity being only one component of that goal.

A noted scholar, Pinker, and a supportive principal fell easy prey to dualistic thinking; certainly the phenomenon is at work in the collective mind of the American psyche as well. Even for people who should know better, urban legend, especially when accompanied by numbers and popularized scientific evidence, carries the weight of truth: Whole language has failed our children! John Dewey and the progressives destroyed our schools! South Carolina's schools are 49th in the nation!

Yet matters are far more complex than the legends or the accompanying numbers.

• • •

Now, I think here we can slip back further than Darwin, to our religious roots as Americans and begin to see how the 5-year-old mind of American society developed, notably in regards to our perception of numbers and science. Religion by its very nature—I do not state this as a value judgment, only as a description—is dogmatic. Religious doctrine states absolutes that are not debatable and are universal, for all and for all time. Pure science, in contrast to vulgar scientism, is organic, changing as the empirical evidence suggests (Raymo, 1998).

While religious beliefs in America are diverse and complex, I believe if we look at the public religion of Americans, the general nexus of American belief, as we have with the American perception of science, we see a strong tendency for black-and-white thinking, dogmatic ideas, and a deep impact on perceptions of the scientific world.

Yes, science and religion have been adversaries for as long as the two collided on the human stage—Is the earth flat? What is the center of the universe? In America, however, a strange paradox has evolved. While the fundamentalists still rail against evolution and other science that seems to deny their faith, the religious part of the American psyche has created its own form of science. At one point, religion saw science as the anti-religion, but in more recent times, religion has manufactured its own scientific self to combat secular science, science of the mere physical world.

• • •

Having taught curriculum and methods courses for many years, I had played more and more with the idea that a religious distinction (in contrast with a scientific bent) can predict a person's stance on issues of curriculum. Discussing the tension between science and religion, Raymo (1998) identifies that conflict in broad terms:

> We are a culture divided at its heart. We warmly embrace the technological and medical fruits of science, but often hold religious beliefs that stand in flat-out contradiction to the scientific way of knowing. (p. 7)

In a language arts methods course, I tossed out my theory in relation to education: People who believe humans to be basically good or innocent lean toward open-ended curriculum and constructivistic theory; people who believe humans to be basically born with sin (Original Sin) embrace more prescriptive curriculum and behavioristic learning theory. In other words, Raymo's general distinction between Skeptics and True Believers offers some explanation for our central debates in education.

I was surprised at a resounding agreement from one student. She had been educated as an undergraduate at a local fundamentalist Christian college. From there, the course discussions often wandered back to issues of religion, ideas, and education. Another important debate developed also concerning "theory" and "belief." This key distinction, to me, contributes a great deal to our discussion here about numbers, science, religion, and education—and the politics of how we teach and test.

Not only do Americans embrace both a vulgar scientism and think collectively in black-and-white dualities, but also Americans have washed away in the popular discourse the distinction between "theory" and "belief." Creationism is no longer simply a stance of the religious; it has become its own science, with scientists and ideas based on data from both scripture and the empirical world of traditional science. That facet of creationism has aided in the refuting of evolution as the sole explanation for human origins (creationism belongs in science courses, they argue, as a competing scientific theory), and it has supported a much more subtle, and corrupting, argument that evolutionary theory is mere belief itself.

Have a glimpse at what I am discussing. Huse (1993), in a work originally published in 1983, argues that creationism is more legitimate than evolution as a theory of the origin of humans. One brief example from his argument here: on page 161, he lists "all of the known scientific facts that can be used to prove evolution"; the page is blank.

• • •

While I would never want to oversimplify or dramatize the mind of today's American when compared to some ideal or distorted image of that mind in the past, some evidence today does suggest a swell in a particularly fundamentalist view of the world in America. Kristof (2003) in the *New York Times* accounted that polling showed nearly half of Americans claiming to be evangelical or born-again Christians, suggesting a fundamentalist streak. Further, and more supporting of this discussion so far, about half of Americans accept creationism, with only 28% accepting evolution. An even more startling comparison is that in 2003, 68% of Americans believe in the devil, more than 2 times greater than those who accept evolutionary theory.

From high school students to well-educated adults, few people can or will distinguish between *belief* based on religious doctrine and scripture and *theory* based on empirical evidence, the scientific method, and peer review. Why? Dualistic thinking will not allow the two to exist in the same realm of truth; in other words, most people see the creationism/evolution debate much like the phonics/whole language debates; the two sides are mutually exclusive. Data, then, usually in the form of numbers, has become the default way to make these somewhat silly arguments. The reduced view of the power of numbers in America is further reinforced by our lingering weakness for the mystical powers of numbers.

Abracadabra—The Magical Power of Numbers

We are in a new millennium. And we mention that fact quite often, as if our measurement of years is anything other than the arbitrary thing it is. But our obsession with decades, centuries, and millennia helps reveal our odd belief in the magical power of numbers, a belief in the mystical that seems to grow from both religious and secular roots.

I think that it is no exaggeration to say that virtually everyone on the planet who celebrated the recent clicking into the 21st century did so exactly one year too early. You see, we have some sort of massive disconnect concerning years; somehow *zero* is more powerful than our collective ability to count. Of course, our powerful friend the computer helped some with that recent confusion, but, nonetheless, a worldwide celebration over an easily measured change of date is quite revealing about the mystical power of numbers on a large scale.

As we approached the new millennium, I was one of the whining sticklers for fact, and I took every opportunity in every class I taught from high school through graduate courses to raise the issue that January 1, 2000, was not the beginning of the new millennium; January 1, 2001, was. Amazingly, time and again, I was resoundingly attacked as wrong, even when I showed the demonstrable fact that I was right.

The most common example that I used stemmed from people's lack of understanding of *zero* and the concept of *counting*. With years, just as with money, dollars, we begin counting with the number one. There is no zero dollar bill and there is no year zero since zero is a place holder, not a serial number. Sorry.

As odd as it looks to most people, our decades, centuries, and millennia end on the last day of years ending in zero, and the new phase begins on the first day of the year ending in one. So a strange phenomenon occurs; the decade of the 1980s actually began on January 1, 1981, and ended on December 31, 1990. Weird but true because the first decade began on January 1, 1, and ended December 31, 10 (in the abstract of course since we labeled such years far after the fact) with the next decade beginning January 1, 11.

If you like, get 1,000 dollar bills and lay them out in 100 rows of 10 and count out loud; then you see the years in front of you. If you need further help, pretend when the bill is lying face up that the leftmost edge is January 1 and the rightmost edge is December 31. See?

Of course, I am being a bit dramatic here; but I was greatly influenced during that time by the clear disconnect between provable phenomenon and more or less intuitive associations with numbers—and even more struck by the powerlessness of *teaching* in the face of such magical associations.

So why did most of the entire world, including most Americans, celebrate the new millennium on the wrong date? How could an educated and sophisticated people make such an easily refuted mistake? I believe it was a combination of several factors that grow from our belief in the mystical power of numbers magnified this time around (you see, in the year 1000 and in the year 1900, the same nonsense occurred concerning Apocalyptic fears) with our panic over Y2K.

That's right. Our friend the computer certainly helped exacerbate our fear of the year 2000; our trepidation that an arbitrary date somehow linked to a fundamentalist Christian belief in the Second Coming and the Apocalyptic end days could itself *cause* anything to happen not of our own making.

Of course Y2K was not mere fabrication like the simple numbering of years from some arbitrary point in the past; basing the date on Jesus' birth seems to be off by anywhere from a few years to a decade or more anyway. Y2K was a real concern that highlights for us our dependence on computers, but also ironically fueled our somewhat childlike fear of magical numbers. Somehow, the American psyche seemed to reason, God was working through the computer to herald the end of humanity.

Neither Y2K nor the year 2000 brought about an Apocalypse, either secular or religious. But the millennium phenomenon does show the workings of the American psyche in broad terms. We believe in quantifying with numbers, such as years; we believe numbers have power, even somewhat mystical powers of causation; and we are strongly influenced in our view of numbers by our religious beliefs, even when those beliefs seem to be in conflict with scientific thought, with observable phenomenon.

• • •

As in the previous section about the religious dogmatism in the American psyche, I have seen more and more evidence that religious beliefs heavily impact how Americas view numbers from minor issues such as years to the more significant flurry of numbers surrounding our schools.

On successive days in my local newspaper, two stories jumped out at me that reinforce my suspicion. The first story concerns Kentucky Mountain Bible College and its phone number; the second, a call for prayer on 3/3/03.

Kentucky Mountain Bible College, it seems, was cursed with a 666 prefix for their phone number. Of course, since 666 is popularly associated with an Apocalyptic significance, a bible college couldn't live with the prefix. It took months, but the college successfully received 693 in its stead. I wonder if anyone pointed out that 693 when added as single digits equals 18 just as 666 does? That's another news article I suppose.

Just one day after the 666 bible college story, the Sunday edition of the paper carried the annual *Parade* issue on salaries, the cover blanketed with 31 small headshots and the salaries for each person with the profession listed. We are what we earn.

In the paper itself, another religious number story ran for that particular date, 3/3/03. Since the date was fairly symmetrical, 3/3/03, a number of religious leaders initiated e-mail campaigns for a day of prayer in recognition of the significance of the number 3 as the trinity in Christianity.

• • •

Several years ago, each time my wife, daughter, and I would eat buffet at a local pizza place, the total would be $13.34. When I paid with a $20, the change would be $6.66, popping up on the screen of the cash register. Once, the girl behind the register screamed and tossed the change she was beginning to count when she glanced at the number.

Without much reflection or skepticism, we tend to imbue numbers that are mere coincidences, that are arbitrary designations, with significances and powers that are beyond symbolic and at least somewhat mystical.

• • •

The religious significances of 3 and 666 are joined by the unlucky number in our culture, 13. Derived from the "bad luck" of Jesus being the 13th at table during the Last Supper, the number 13 is the most common number with negative connotations; many people have idiosyncratic distastes for or fear of numbers.

Does it make any sense that Friday the 13th can actually *cause* mishap? That 3 is somehow holy? That 666 can or will herald the doom of humanity? Only when the numbers are interpreted as they are by the mainstream American psyche, that odd mix of religious belief and vulgar scientism that makes numbers powerful.

"It's the Economy, Stupid"— Numbers and Money in America

Then, of course in America, there is money—"making money," as we say. We may speak of democratic values, but we live for the pursuit of capital. That we are a nation more committed *in behavior* to capitalism than democracy helps reinforce in our minds the value of numbers. Our capitalistic assumptions tell us this: Numbers are value-laden, and they must be earned.

When the George W. Bush administration spoke out against the University of Michigan's admission policy that awarded 20 points (notably, the opponents emphasized, higher points than the 12 possible points given for SAT scores) for selected ethnicities, a majority of Americans objected to the policy. The *Detroit Free Press* reported that polls of residents of Michigan rejected the policy at 63%; interestingly, they also opposed the 20 points awarded by Michigan for being a legacy, a relative of an alumnus, a policy common at universities for decades. (It may be relevant to note that the legacy policy was a benefit afforded President Bush upon his college entrance.)

That polls show an equal distaste for both the race-based *and* legacy policies suggests that race may not be at the heart of American's balking at awarding points for status instead of awarding points for performance. The 12-point possibility for the SAT seems to come under virtually no scrutiny from the public, although higher education has fired significant shots at the credibility of the test, which we will discuss later.

The University of Michigan controversy suggests to me that Americans often equate numbers with value, analogous to the value placed on money. Our capitalistic grounding as Americans raises our skepticism when people appear to get something of value for no effort. At least in the last 20 years, we have seen a similar phenomenon with a growing rejection of welfare programs, not because we don't want to help the needy, but because we *perceive* the programs as dominated by those getting something for nothing (although that perception may itself not be accurate, it certainly is believed).

• • •

While I believe the American psyche is both enamored by and dedicated to the power of numbers, I also see that phenomenon as incredibly complex and multifaceted. We have committed to a vulgar scientism that is somewhat oddly reinforced by our religious tendencies and our lingering vulnerability to the mystical. Though these elements are strong and significant, I think our capitalism, our belief in market ideology and consumerism, cannot be underestimated as it impacts how we think about numbers and how (or if) we value public education.

At no other time in history has such a push to supplant public education as an institution been so directly challenged by the promise of competition-based private education. Michael Engel (2000) discusses *The Struggle for Control of Public Education* and begins the argument by noting America's allegiance to market ideology, to capitalism at the expense of democracy. Here he believes direct relationships exist between "the dominance of quantitative measurements," the proliferation of numbers, and "[m]arket ideology . . .[as they have] triumphed over democratic values" (pp. 8–9). Education, he argues, has become mired in "human-capital theory," resulting in students' "value [being] measured in dollars, not in their humanity"—those numbers ultimately meaning more than people (p. 35).

Lewis (2003), among others, recognizes that we have begun to fashion a strange and conflicting view of students as products along with our growing view of parents and students as consumers. Both

Engel and Lewis see this capitalistic ideology as antithetical to democracy, which, they would argue, must be sustained through public education:

> Those who still believe in the worth and possibilities of the common public school need to say so. And they ought first to pledge never to refer to a student as a product. (Lewis, 2003, p. 564)

• • •

And, too, there is the value of teachers.

I taught public education for nearly two decades. During that time, I published widely and regularly; eventually I earned a doctorate in education—all the while teaching full-time at a high school, coaching soccer at that same school, and teaching as an adjunct at several local colleges and universities. Over that part of my career, I amassed some respect and wonderful experiences within my field.

During the entire 18 years, when anyone meeting me asked what I did for a living, my answer, that I was a high school English teacher, usually elicited an "O" that suggested, "I'm sorry." Then I took an assistant professorship at a local and prestigious university, one close enough to my home that I did not have to move. Each and every time I came in contact with people for the first time after my career change, I experienced the same response, "Wow, you're at Furman now. You enjoying that big raise?"

Then the ugly part. Each time I have to explain that I took a significant pay cut to move from public education to higher education. At first, they all laugh; they think I am joking. After I convince them that I am being sincere, they come back with the familiar, "Oh." It was not the prestige of the university or of being a college professor; their initial good cheer was based on an assumption of a big pay check—no, a *bigger* pay check.

If you make a lot of money in America, you must be worth something. If you don't, or you are stupid enough to take a pay cut, something must be wrong. Similar to Engel's point about capitalism and democracy in the American psyche, dollars matter more than the actual worth of one's profession in the good ol' U. S. of A.

• • •

When Engel's discussion is seen within the context of my arguments so far, market ideology begins to fit neatly into the flaw of dualistic thinking running through vulgar scientism and dogmatic religiosity. The best of public education would spring from democratic values, Engel (2000) believes, not the dehumanizing and reductionistic nature of market ideology (pp. 52–53).

Capitalism as a prime component of the American psyche, I believe, is the central secular driving force stirring the array of *ways of thinking* in the American mind that directly clings to numbers and the power of numbers to measure and mandate what our schools should teach and how we should teach students. Further, capitalism contributes heavily to the dehumanization of people within the schools. Test scores and tax dollars spent swirl through the system as if people are not there, much like the house flooded with binary code in the home security commercial. In the American psyche, we may actually be more concerned about protecting the house and all the valuables while completely forgetting that people live there.

• • •

The American capitalistic impulse also is often oversimplified in the broad context of the American psyche. We have a fairly sloppy (or at least monolithic) understanding of supply and demand, the free-market paradigm, and the role of consumers. Our oversimplification of capitalism within the free-market system has its own pitfalls, but when those narrow understandings are then transposed onto public education, we have a scenario that can only fail students and ultimately a free democracy.

Money matters, and the competition model in business is the central paradigm, our society claims, that maintains the balance of a free-market economy. Thus, public education is condemned for being a monopoly, placing it afoul of the tenets of the competition model. That argument (a false one, I argue) contributes to a distorted and simplistic view of consumers and their roles.

Let's stay within the private business world for a moment. The role of the consumer is not monolithic in the business world. There exists a profound difference in the fast-food consumer or the motorist in search of cheap gasoline and *consumers who purchase the services of experts.* Two examples can serve this point—one concerning medical doctors and one concerning club soccer.

If consumers of expert advice or services behave with the "boss" mentality ("I am paying you so you do as I say"), a mentality that is perfectly appropriate in some aspects of free-market consumer/business interactions, both the consumer and the expert are cheated in the transaction. For example, if parents take their sick child to a medical doctor and pay for his services, the entire exchange is corrupted if the consumers (parents and child) demand that the doctor treat the child by the laying on of hands, even if the parents believe this will cure the child. This subsumes the expertise of the doctor with the whims of the consumer. Likewise, demanding the prescribing of antibiotics is equally corrupting. (Remember the hypothetical twins from earlier in the chapter?)

A less dramatic example, but a common one, is the paying of soccer coaches in club soccer. On every team I have been involved with as a parent or an assistant coach, the head coach explains up front that even though the parents are paying him, he makes all the coaching decisions; that is his area of expertise. A coach cannot function successfully under a system that allows nonexpert consumers to override his expertise, the exact service he is being paid to perform.

Yet, this idea of "consumer as boss" (echoed in the not-so-distant past by Ross Perot's populist run for president in which he portrayed the running of a democracy in the business paradigm) is the exact model being foisted onto education within the context of quantitative measurement of student, teacher, and school performances along with cost-effective dispensing of education in a competition-based system of private education.

With the medical and soccer examples in mind, also consider how we tend to assess the abilities of professionals and experts; medical doctors police themselves, and soccer coaches license themselves, experts policing experts to maintain the integrity of the profession. In that powerful world of science, "scientists declare that their profession has properly policed itself" through peer review (Gould, 1996, p. 87; Raymo, 1998). Yet with education, we are choosing an inappropriate capitalistic model—consumer as boss in a competition paradigm—instead of allowing educators to monitor their own profession.

• • •

A key component of our numbers games is our capitalistic resolve, a very narrow and inappropriate one for education. An urge to quantify, to measure, and to assign value exists in our business world and has crept into education throughout the last 100 years. Adrienne Rich (2001) fears that public education has fallen victim to this poisoning capitalistic influence:

> Universal public education has two possible—and contradictory—missions. One is the development of a literate, articulate, and well-informed citizenry so that the democratic process can continue to evolve and the promise of radical equality can be brought closer to realization. The other is the per-

petuation of a class system dividing an elite, nominally "gifted" few, tracked from an early age, from a very large underclass essentially to be written off as alienated from language and science, from poetry and politics, from history and hope—toward low-wage temporary jobs. The second is the direction our society has taken. (p. 162)

And we should not think Rich's fears are unfounded, or mere leftist rhetoric. In Texas (so much happens in Bush's home state concerning education), private philanthropists and businesses are now paying students and teachers for passing AP exams ("Texas students," 2003). This mix of money, business, and standardized testing offers at least some potential for corrupting this thing called learning. Further, it reinforces the value of external motivation at the expense of learning for the sake of learning. With our schools, America has spoken loud and clear: We love capitalism with democracy relegated to lip service at best.

Majorities Rule, Don't They?

Henry David Thoreau (1962) mused about "a majority of one" (p. 93), but the current American perception of and value of democracy and majority rule are a far cry from those romantic days when America still wrestled publicly about the role of government and democracy. We are consumers first; democracy and our participation in it now simply swirl invisibly through our lives.

Yet, polling and voting are our most tangible and quantified manifestations of democracy, although I would argue again that ours is a corruption of democratic ideals, a corruption from oversimplification by numbers, by measurement. Americans do have a certain affinity for majority opinions, and I would say we are a bit callous about minority views. Simply consider the backlash against the antiwar voice when the U.S. invaded Iraq under George W. Bush, oil man and name behind the No Child Left Behind education initiative. But most disturbing is that democracy has been virtually subsumed by our drive for capital. The quest for money now threatens our most essential democratic institution—public schools.

• • •

Engel (2000) makes a solid case for the prominence of market ideology in American thought, but he also shows the *need* for a recommitment to democracy and democratic foundations such as public schools. In Engel's discussion, we can see the complexity of democratic ideology: Jeffersonian ideas of public education supporting the survival of American democracy, Deweyan and pragmatic calls for democracy as a way of living, and the holistic and chaotic nature of democracy as a rejection of dualistic and reductionistic thought. That complexity at the center of American democracy has been supplanted by the reductionistic nature of both American vulgar scientism (the drive to quantify through measurement) and our market ideology, our capitalistic zeal.

For capitalistic ideology to remain king in the American psyche, we can speculate, public education must be eradicated since it is the key institution to fuel complex democratic principles:

> A democratic school is one that, above all, tries to enable people to create their own world collectively rather than fit into one that is created for them. (Engel, 2000, p. 65)

As we continue to explore our numbers games, the political cycle that controls our schools, we have to keep in mind Engel's recognition that *a public school system based on democratic principles is also a revolutionary institution*, as it emphasizes the essential conflict that exists in the cultural wars that are fought on school grounds at the expense of children in America.

• • •

Ultimately, our schools are run as fiefdoms—places where students and teachers alike are relatively powerless and voiceless, where most all activity is quantified (thus removing any faces from teaching and learning). When schools are driven by market ideology and capitalistic assumptions, then schooling is done *to* students, not *with* or *for* students. Numbers have reduced the American grasp on democracy, a complex and ever-changing process of becoming, and nowhere is that corruption more disturbingly displayed than in our public schools. This is a phenomenon that is accelerating as I write this book.

We're Number One!

Think about the Olympics. As good Americans, we cheer for the Red, White, and Blue, and as good Americans, we demand gold medals, nothing less than being Number One. And for most of us, we consider that second person or team losers because it is the winning that counts.

I've seen dozens of athletes hang their heads in shame—for being second. All that effort, that journey to the competition, the *act* of competing reduced to nothingness because it is the winning that counts. Number One.

The American psyche is grounded in valuing the ends over the means. We are a finish-line society, not a journey society. This mentality of winning, of achieving Number-One status appears to be a lofty one, one that drives us to be successful. In fact, it is the basis of our standard cry in education, a cry that has occurred over and over throughout the past century. Yet when placed in the context of learning and teaching, our ends mentality is doing us more harm than good.

• • •

The tension—and ultimately harm—existing between a finish-line mentality and a journey mentality has its roots in some of the early and great voices in educational debate, Boyd Bode and John Dewey. Engel (2000) quotes both, revealing the nature of learning and teaching as they conflict with the static nature of end-product thinking:

> In the words of Bode, it is "neither a matter of developing faculties nor of forming apperceptive masses according to a fixed procedure. If we keep our eye on the fact that learning is a reconstruction of experience, which is a distinctive thing in the case of each individual pupil, we avoid the danger of mechanizing the learning process. . . ."

> What then is education for? "Since growth is the characteristic of life," says Dewey, "education is all one with growing; it has no end beyond itself. . . ." Dewey . . . makes it clear that he is talking about a certain kind of growth: a development of intellectual skills and personal attitudes needed to build a democratic society. (p. 57)

The magic and power associated with being Number One, being the best—as opposed to the journey, the striving to grow—can only corrupt the teaching/learning process since the status of ranking, attaining number one, is ends-oriented and teaching and learning are journeys without an end, except as they coincide with death. As Dewey argued, living and learning are inherently inseparable. I would add that quantifying either is both misleading and undesirable.

• • •

At about the same time that I entered the teaching profession, I became a serious cyclist, eventually racing for many years. My wife throughout those years was a runner; she often stepped out the front door and ran 8 or 10 miles, just to run 8 or 10 miles. You see, she never raced, and I can't really remember her keeping that much track of her time.

By the mid 1990s, I caught the running bug and trained for two marathons in 1995. I also entered other running races and events. What struck me immediately about shifting to the running world was the exact split I noted above; cyclists tended to be ends-oriented (Did you win? Who did you beat?), while runners were primarily focused on self-competition, concerned mainly with personal best times. Runners are often complimenting each other on reaching their best times, regardless of that time's comparison with anyone else's time.

My point? Learning and teaching are about the becoming, about reaching one's personal best only to strive to pass that mark again (Rogers, 1995). Learning is competing with one's self during a journey that never ends.

• • •

And then there is school. Rimer (2003) reports that "some students are more focused on their grade-point averages than on what they might be learning." And we wonder why? The ends-oriented mentality of America combined with the test-driven school system more or less insure such a superficial and counter-educational result for our students. The numbers matter; the learning does not. And Number One? It seems that the quest for valedictorian—as a ticket to higher education, a voucher to be cashed—has created students who '"know how to do schools,'" but offer little else of real value in the real world.

If Numbers Predict, Then Why Play the Game?

For the average person, seeing numbers from test scores in the newspaper shows proof of the overall quality of teaching and learning in schools, districts, and the state; direct cause and effect relationships; and accurate portrayals of reality. In short, we see numbers as irrefutable facts of existence, not as statistical facts (to be discussed in the next section). "Jessi scored 1240 on her SAT" is a significant fact of her existence, but "Jessi is a global thinker and needs the big picture first" is merely an opinion and doesn't really count for much, or so the average person assumes.

But how true are those assumptions based merely on numbers? Once we have data on a grade level in a particular school, the average person sees that as predictive for the next group of students in the grade level; actually we begin to assume that one class's score is predictive of the expectation for the next group to score higher, without exception. And here is where one problem with quantitative data comes in, commonly referred to as comparing apples to oranges.

Yes, statisticians have worked for decades to improve the comparisons of different populations, but we all know that at best, such a comparison is a tenuous act. Further, we also know that in many schools the populations of differing students is so small that the comparison becomes less and less credible. Yet, we need those numbers, but we also need to admit the flaws with such numbers and to acknowledge further the superiority of narrative, qualitative accounts of those populations for the purposes of describing, evaluating, and improving instruction. Qualitative assessments can identify the idiosyncrasies of reality in ways that numbers cannot.

Not only do we use numbers to guide our assumption for continual improvement of *groups* (another oversimplification, here of social Darwinistic thinking) among different populations (in contrast to the previous discussion for self-competition for personal growth as a state of becoming), but also we have a culturally simplistic understanding of cause and effect, often confused with correlations. When I discuss the SAT with students, I make sure they are aware of the high historical positive correlations between socioeconomic status of a child's family and the level of education of that child's parents with SAT scores. What do they always assume? That those factors *cause* the scores by students. This careless and dangerous assumption of cause and effect when dealing with quantitative data is at the heart of every educational research study portrayed in newspapers across America. Simplified data drawn from complex endeavors that are displayed for a nonprofessional audience in a simplistic manner can only be more deceptive than informative. In short, beware tables displaying test results in the newspaper. Correlations are relatively easy to reveal, but drawing conclusions about cause and effect is extremely complex and fraught with pitfalls.

• • •

Let's make a quick analogy. Recently, I listened to a national radio morning show discuss the trend of the Greenbay Packers defeating the Chicago Bears in NFL football. As noted before, sports in America is inundated with numbers. But pro teams are like classes of students—when the students themselves or the players themselves shuffle, the performance of the group next year in a unique performance *cannot* be predicted. The simple truth is twofold. Statistical data on the past cannot predict; that data is *descriptive* of a past phenomenon and it does hold some value, though prediction is not one of them. Statistical data on performances by unique populations is *not* the same as taking a poll before an election. If polling is done well, it can predict quite accurately. Comparing two separate performances by diverse groups of humans, though, is not polling.

Second, and I might argue more importantly, the performances themselves are far more vital than the *potential* for those performances. In the real world, it is quite possible that a Packers defeat of the Bears by 14–7 this season is in actuality a better performance than a defeat of the Bears 37–0 the year before. As well, the 2003 scores of a third-grade class might be lower on average than the scores of the 2002 third-grade class, yet the 2003 class performed better. How? The 2003 scores were far above the performances of that same class in the past, but the 2002 scores were below the performances of that class in the past.

In human endeavors such as sports and teaching and learning, *potential* will always pale to actual *performance*. And each unique performance by an individual or a group is just that, unique. Numbers may serve us well to attempt standardization, but that attempt is at least distorting if not completely undesirable.

Numbers don't lie, I guess, but they certainly are a source of vast misunderstandings. Hence, let's look now at the truth, the whole truth, and nothing but the truth.

A Tale of Three Truths—
Poetic, Historical, and Statistical

A former student of mine made a confession to me once; she uses information from novels to support her arguments with people. She admitted to me that she referenced Barbara Kingsolver's *The Poisonwood Bible* to make her points in a religion debate with a friend.

She added that a novel gave her *awareness*, and for her, awareness is far more valuable, and more complicated, than mere facts or quantifying numbers. Yes, poetic truths stand in stark contrast to the ap-

parent desire a culture has for simple truths such as "Just Say No" or
"Four out of five dentists prefer. . . ."

In the American mind, as I have attempted to show, all things that
are quantifiable are truths. But if our goal of schooling is to serve a
democracy and each individual well, a variety of truths must be embraced. Those truths for this discussion will be called *poetic, historical,*
and *statistical.*

• • •

What is the value of a painting by Salvador Dalí? A poem by
Adrienne Rich? The Coen brothers' film *Raising Arizona*? What does
art contribute?

This is the domain of *poetic truth*—truth that is relative and complicated, and often only metaphorically connected with the real
world. In some ways, poetic truth is the antithesis of numbers that
quantify. As an English teacher for years, I had to fight the constant
urge we have as humans to reduce art to themes, which are simply
numbers games with words. As I argued that playing the game is
more important than the potential for the game, I would argue as vo-
ciferously that the work of art as a whole *is* its meaning, not some reduction of that art to a theme or moral. But even when truth comes to
us in metaphor—these images, these words, these events are as *if* they
happened, as *if* they existed, and are therefore telling us truth, though
not *the* truth—we are driven to reduce it.

Barbara Kingsolver may very well show us in *The Poisonwood Bible*
that religiosity is a slippery thing, but it is the whole book, the events
and characters, as it is read and after it is read, and discussed with
others, that has meaning. Being Number One on the best-seller list or
stating its theme adds nothing to that reading. So by its nature, poetic
truth is complicated and ephemeral; and more often than not it raises
questions instead of answering them.

• • •

As a society, America values poetic truth very little; we treat art
and those truths from art as mere add-ons, so much fluff. In school
we view the arts as electives, or extras. In society, we ironically pay
some artists huge sums of money in the music and movie industries,
but even then, it is as entertainers, not as those who give us the truths
we need to live; the artists who offer substance often starve.

A bit further up the food chain in the American psyche is *historical
truth*, those events and people who have populated this planet and
left some sort of mark. Historical truth in America again shows our

tendency to reduce and politicize even those things that are fairly easy to identify. While art is often reduced to themes and morals in our classrooms, schools and society enjoy simplifying and spinning key events and people of history—especially when those events or people may help drive a political agenda, may serve as proof of what we wish to be true.

Take our Founding Fathers as just one example. No group of men in history have displayed a greater range of complexities and contradictions than the group we have come to call Founding Fathers—Benjamin Franklin, George Washington, Thomas Jefferson, just to mention some of the most commonly cited Fathers. Yes, Americans clearly value history and tradition far more than art, but we value history in its reduced and politicized forms, just as we have corrupted the meaning of "science," distorting and misapplying the value of numbers that quantify.

Again, that America as a collective creates myth from history shows our tendency to think as a whole with the 5-year-old mind. We take Thoreau's "simplify" to a perverse extreme. Few days have gone by in the past 20 years without someone somewhere stating that our Founding Fathers based this country on the word of God, implying often and directly stating occasionally that most of these mythologized men were somehow traditional, orthodox Christians, possibly even fundamentalist in their beliefs.

In the American climate, though, show those people letters and writings by any of the Fathers—Franklin, Washington, and Jefferson serve us well here again—proving that most of the Founding Fathers were Deists, that many were agnostic or atheists, and that they all were men of reason who would today easily be called humanists, and then watch such demonstrable facts be resoundingly denied, much like the silly millennium celebration. As with numbers, we like our history neatly bleached and starched. Depictions of Santa Claus and Jesus often reflect the culture creating the depiction; our Founding Fathers' ideas suffer that same fate, neatly poured into the dogmatic jar of the time.

• • •

And then—*statistical truth*. With these three arbitrary areas of truth, we need to consider how they mesh with reality. Poetic truth comes from those things existing *as if* they are a part of reality; historical truth, which carries the weight of "fact" that poetic truth does not, springs from real events and real people, although those facts of reality may be greatly distorted by perception and by expression. Statistical truth is the human drive to capture reality in numbers.

We will discuss later how statistics intertwine with the politics of education, but first we need to briefly wrestle with how numbers represent reality. Here is a simple example. A room of 10 people take out all their money and add the amount, the total being $140. We can say with statistical certainty that each person in the room has an *average* of $14. Much like the date of the beginning of a new millennium or Jefferson's letters rejecting Christ's Virgin Birth, that average is a fact, a statistical fact. Yet if we go back to those 10 people, the reality may be that 9 people had no money, while 1 person had the entire $140. Two truths, one the reality and one statistical, exist simultaneously.

Yes, we know that small populations make such statistical truths less likely to reflect reality, but the point is that statistical truth is at best a reduction of reality and at worst a distortion. If the average family in America has 2.4 children, then there actually exists *no* average family since .4 of a child doesn't exist. Further, as we will explore in the next chapter, as with historical truth, political manipulation of statistical truth is alive and well in contemporary America.

When George W. Bush began pushing a tax cut, both the left and the right manipulated a certain view of numbers to make their political ideology shine. Republicans enjoyed stating *average* tax cut amounts; while Democrats preferred to isolate specific wage earners' tax cuts. Both sides were telling statistical truths that existed simultaneously and accurately, because, well, numbers don't lie, to make their skewed ideological point.

Counting on the American Psyche

I have drawn here a Frankenstein of sorts, a piecemeal creature I call the American psyche. The various parts ultimately work as one whole, though some parts seem to contrast sharply with others—until the unifying urge to simplify and politicize is worked into the equation.

This Frankenstein has a 5-year-old mind that embraces a quantifying science; values dogma; imbues numbers with magical qualities; worships market ideology while giving democracy lip service; and holds up truth as long as it is simple and serves the ideology of a political agenda that never bends. Think of it as a Teflon®-coated philosophy that no complex evidence will stick to. And who loves this Frankenstein? Politicians and journalists do. And for decades they have conspired (often an ironic conspiracy, I admit) to let loose this monster, turning our schools into the most horrifying haunted houses.

Gould (1996) recognizes "the particular prestige of numbers and the special difficulty that their refutation entails"; thus, Americans are drawn to "analyzing quantitative data" and "the special status that numbers enjoy" (p. 58). Yes, numbers are alluring because they feel true—especially when they seem to confirm what we *wish* to be true, especially when we have our assumptions confirmed by science: "The mystique of science proclaims that numbers are the ultimate test of objectivity," Gould explains (p. 58). What we are about to explore is the power that those *in* power can wield when they hide their agendas, hide their ideologies behind that "special status that numbers enjoy."

# TWO

○○
Politics, Media, and Education—
Honesty among the Numbers

Recently, I tuned into my local AM talk-radio show. The late after-noon host has adopted education as a hobby of his. To be accurate, his hobby is proclaiming loudly the wasteful spending of taxpayer money on public education (we have too many teachers, not too few; and class size is too low, not too high, he explains) and the irrefutable fact that schools can be saved by one simple thing—vouchers, school choice, the good ol' competition model. As I will show later in Chapter Four, much of the motivation behind numbers games lies in a desire to discredit schools so the American public will choose choice and abandon public education to embrace privatized schooling. Like gas stations, there is money to be made in schools.

On this particular afternoon, the host had a board member from the largest school district in South Carolina in the studio to discuss a study commissioned by the board to compare schools in that district with like-schools across the entire state; apparently the district rated poorly in a study that ranked schools within socioeconomic categories by state-testing scores, the Palmetto Achievement Challenge Test (PACT).

The discussion and conclusions drawn by the board member (a lawyer) and the host (a broadcaster/journalist by training) were all based on *never seeing the actual report*, only the rankings without the data producing the rankings, and were replete with broad generalizations such as the host saying that the study *proved* clearly (scientifically, of course) that teacher pay and student-teacher ratios do not matter. Further, again based merely on a ranking and not the body of evidence gathered in the actual study, they began a lengthy discussion of the need for ability-grouping in classes.

I immediately engaged the host in a series of e-mails explaining the inability to draw valid conclusions without seeing the study, the lack of research supporting many of their generalizations, their complete lack of knowledge of how the schools were being run in the county (schools still tend to group by ability, especially in math and language arts, but they were blaming *heterogeneous* grouping for the poor performances), and mostly their simplistic approaches to the entire discussion—simplistic approaches grounded in assumptions about numbers and about statistical data, simplistic approaches driven more by capitalistic ideology than educational expertise. Despite my being a veteran public school teacher, despite my holding a doctorate in curriculum and instruction, and despite my expertise in the fields they were discussing, I was harshly dismissed as an educrat. Because numbers don't lie, but educrats do.

• • •

Politicians, journalists, and pundits may or may not be overtly aware of American perceptions of numbers, science, and such, but without a doubt, they are consistently manipulating those perceptions (see Raymo, 1998, for a discussion of such a phenomenon in issues concerning science and religion). Their favorite football in that political game is our education system; it has all the right ingredients—the appeal of helping children, the anchor of being tax-funded, the stench of socialism, and a tradition steeped in testing and number gathering. The role of the media is central to this debate. Referring to the National Commission on Excellence in Education, which gave us *A Nation at Risk*, in the 1980s, Goodlad (2003) notes that "media overkill turned attention away from [the report's] substance." That single instance, however, is typical of the educational discussion that routinely takes place in America.

Throughout the conversations concerning education, the voices that are loudest tend to be people who have little or no training in education as a discipline, people who have little or no experience as educators, and people who have political and ideological agendas and see education as a means of promoting those agendas. In this chapter we will look at a drama that has played out over a century—one involving politicians, journalists, pundits, the average

American on the street, and education professionals (those who are practitioners and those whose area of scholarship and training is education). The never-ending educational debate, of course, depends heavily on numbers, the sweet certainty of numbers.

• • •

As he wrestled with the credibility of IQ, Gould (1996) also swam in waters similar to my discussion—the nature of science, the power of numbers, the role of media and laypeople as we interpret research and numbers. About science and numbers:

> Science is rooted in creative interpretation. Numbers suggest, constrain, and refute; they do not, by themselves, specify the content of scientific theories. Theories are built upon the interpretation of numbers, and interpreters are often trapped by their own rhetoric. They believe in their own objectivity, and fail to discern the prejudice that leads them to one interpretation among many consistent with their numbers. (Gould, 1996, p. 106)

And it is Gould's awareness of the role of the interpreter that is crucial here. Often educational research comes to the average person after being filtered through politicians and the media, virtually none of whom are expert as researchers or educators. When Gould discusses the particularly sloppy public reaction to *The Bell Curve*, he emphasizes that such a book is "a rhetorical masterpiece of scientism, and the particular kind of anxiety and obfuscation that numbers impose upon nonprofessional commentators" (p. 371).

I would add to our discussion Gould's observation that the IQ debate is typical of the education debate writ large. We all should be careful when we are shown research, a plethora of numbers, or are told by a journalist or a politician that *this* or *that* will *certainly* save our failing schools.

Of Research and Data— The Politics of Loving Numbers

At some level, whether conscious or intuitive, politicians, pundits, and those in the media are aware of the American psyche as it behaves as a collective in the terms I presented in the first chapter—our love, our distorted love, of numbers in all their (sometimes baffling) manifestations. Added to that phenomenon are the inherent complexities in the acts of teaching and learning and in the running of public schools. Two issues that make the educational debate virtually unmanageable are the necessarily political nature of a tax-funded entity and the relative lack of clear academic weight in the field called "education."

Within the academic community, primarily within universities and colleges, a long-running tension has existed between departments and colleges of education and the so-called academic departments and colleges, such as English, history, math, or science. Part of the tension revolves around education establishing itself as an academic field. What is the content of education as an academic discipline? What is the research base of the field? Gardner (2002) speaks openly about the problem education has had with establishing its academic credibility, especially in terms of educational research. He notes major works such as Lagemann's *An Elusive Science: The Troubling History of Education Research* and places this problem in the context of *A Nation at Risk* from the mid 1980s under Reagan and No Child Left Behind under the current Bush administration. How does Gardner's point impact this discussion?

Primarily, education as a field has been fighting the American addiction to traditional experimental research that is number-laden, reductionistic, and bound to statistical truth. Concurrently, education has had to contend with the traditional perceptions of professions, notably the medical profession. As the momentum toward more assessment that gathers numerical data, toward quantifying education to insure high standards and to increase accountability has mushroomed, an ironic backlash has begun—one that may save education as a field by establishing its academic integrity in terms of content and research. The numbers games may in fact help to illuminate the humanity of the field called teaching.

This disrespect for teachers and colleges of education may be at a high point today. Keller (2003) explores a report on the "intellectually thin" nature of schools of education: "Mr. Steiner unveiled his research here last month to the delight of those who have long criticized education schools for their low standards." This article reveals a great deal about the *perception* of education as a profession, but if read closely, it also uncovers the ideological drive by researchers today to discredit teacher certification at all costs. And where do these studies get revealed? The neat comfort of local papers, often from the lips of politicians. Baines (2003) laments about this climate:

Although teachers have been given the sacrosanct responsibility of developing the intellectual and social capital of the country, almost anyone can certify teachers—and they do. The education and experience of the adults entrusted to care for our children has become superfluous in relation to what most legislators perceive as more pressing needs, such as vouchers, testing, and more testing.

As we move into the political quagmire surrounding the educational debate and within the educational field, let's add to my argument about the characteristics of the collective American psyche the often ignored current state of educational experts and their stances concerning numbers since this is where we could save public education. Over the last 100 years politicians have held the power in the running of schools, journalists have been the voice for those politicians to the common person, and educational experts and practitioners have remained the entire time outside the debate at best and resoundingly vilified at worst, as Baines (2003) shows in his experience.

• • •

Even among progressive education advocates, the trashing of teacher education and a willingness to line up with those who claim only content knowledge matters in the training of a teacher is gaining momentum. Again, the story unfolds in the papers. Leon Botstein, president of Bard College and author of a challenge to reform high schools across America, unveiled a new teacher certification program at his college with the newly politicized cry "that teachers do not know enough about the subjects they teach" (Arenson, 2003). Botstein's new program fits neatly into the dictates of NCLB—increased content requirements for future teachers, decreased courses in pedagogy, and a claim that teacher licensing programs in the states have an unfair stranglehold on teaching.

While progressive moves such as the one at Bard College should be embraced, we must ask if the move is more political than educational. Also, this announcement fails to address a key issue with teacher certification. It does address an apparent lack of content knowledge by secondary teachers, but what content areas do K–8 teachers need? Most at those levels teach *all* content areas. What do we do there? Regardless, this move by Botstein and Bard College will gain a great deal of attention in the media and will contribute, if nothing else, to the momentum of NCLB dismantling traditional schools of education.

• • •

W. James Popham stands now as one of the top educational experts—notably at the forefront of the measurement movement in American public education—who has watched numbers become politically distorted and who has chosen to enter the political fray. Popham has distinguished himself as a professor and as a key figure and voice in the American Educational Research Association (AERA); in many ways, Popham's name (now ironically) is most often associated with the growth of standardized testing and statistical data in relation to public education. From the educational measurement side, he has made many and significant contributions to the numbers games.

His recent works, however, show a marked stance against the current state of testing and numbers in education (Popham, 1999; Popham, 2001a; Popham, 2001b; Popham, 2003). While his work speaks for itself, I believe Dr. Popham argues several key points that are currently sitting outside the political debate, yet offer the right-minded approach to numbers and how we teach students in our public schools. Broadly, Popham explains that objective standardized testing and our traditional gathering of numerical data concerning schools are both potentially either valuable *or* harmful practices. He warns that unless educators gather and analyze data effectively, we are likely to do more harm than good. The misuse of such testing and data include, according to Popham, teaching to the tests, gathering data for data's sake, improperly drawing evaluations concerning schools and students from data, and essentially allowing lay misunderstandings of assessment, statistics, and instructional and curricular decisions to flourish without the guidance of experienced educators.

While Popham's informed voice is joined by many others (Coles, 2000; Kohn, 2000)—and the volume is increasing, though the stages are few—what public education is faced with is a troubling mix. Pundits have the bully pulpit of talk radio, journalists have the authoritative voice in the educational debate, politicians have all the power for implementing educational practices, and professional educators (from instructional and curricular specialists to testing and measurement experts to classroom practitioners) are forced outside the debate along with students (who have essentially no voice) and their parents (who are being manipulated by being promised a voice, a *choice*, often for reasons that have little to do with teaching and learning).

A New Honesty in Education—
Positivist Measures in a Postmodern World

The debates swirling around education never stray too far from the forefront of key concerns for Americans. In South Carolina, for example, education grew to be a central issue of the 1998 governor's race, the arguments centering on the lottery and video poker versus vouchers and high standards for teachers and students. Concurrent with that political season *The Atlantic* ran a feature article on education, Nicholas Lemann's "'Ready Read!'" applauding Robert E. Slavin's Success for All reading program. Both the SC governor's race and the Lemann article epitomize a central aspect of the current educational debate—dishonesty, ideological dishonesty neatly clothed in numerical armor and played out in the media or in the political arena. That dishonesty runs through almost all the educational discourse and most often involves data in the form of numbers; such dishonesty grows from the clash inherent in the power of positivist measurements, primarily through standardized testing and the quantifying and evaluations drawn from those tests, within a culture that is concurrently influenced by postmodern perspectives at the highest academic and artistic levels.

Since the rise of Taylorism in the business world at the turn of the century, education has been driven by a belief in empirical data, the belief that we can objectively generate meaningful numbers from standardized tests to assess both individual students and entire educational systems—from individual schools to school districts to state-by-state comparisons to the public school system as a whole (Kliebard, 1995, pp. 81–82). Within the last few decades, the academic and scientific communities (Raymo, 1998) have simultaneously developed a skeptical if not somewhat cynical postmodern attitude that such objectivity is a delusion, or at least misleading and oversimplified; Gould (1996) expresses his embracing passion as a scientist and offers a postmodern view of *objectivity*: "Objectivity must be operationally defined as fair treatment of data, not absence of preference," or any absence of humanity, I would add (p. 36).

The result has been that educators function under a Jekyll and Hyde personality, both gathering and displaying huge amounts of empirical data on educational performance while often discounting much of that data as biased or only relatively true; we often explain that the findings are far too complicated for mere politicians, journalists, and parents to understand while we bash journalists for displaying that data in overly simplistic formats, thus misleading that unaware public and fueling political agendas. In short, the majority of Americans still accept the objective truth of empirical data while the intellectual elite harbor a cynicism toward objectivity—though they continue to produce large amounts of experimental and quasi-experimental studies that still carry the greatest weight in the world of research (and has recently received the stamp of approval from the federal government!).

To move beyond this problematic duality, educators speaking with a unified though not monolithic voice must demand educational honesty from the media and within the ongoing political discourse, especially against the high tide of numbers. They must be honest about text books and curriculum programs, they must be honest about standardized testing and statistical data, they must be honest about the nature of educating, and they must be honest with our students in the classroom. In the face of dilemmas influenced by both positivistic and postmodern attitudes, we must strive for a new educational honesty that directly confronts the misconceptions of the American psyche and the ideological agendas of politicians, pundits, and journalists. The people behind all those numbers *will* lie.

• • •

Dishonesty is actually not a new phenomenon in education. Bracey (1997a) and Kliebard (1995), among others, have noted that throughout the 20th century, the American educational debate has been rife with dishonesty when it benefited *either* politicians or educators; both camps have generated and massaged numbers to make their cases. Bracey suggests that since the Reagan years and *A Nation at Risk*, politicians have manipulated for political gain America's love affair with statistics. Kliebard details a philosophical struggle over the American curriculum for the last 100 years, a century dotted with educators fighting for philosophical control of the schools.

Recently, Bracey (2003a) has shown with direct evidence that *A Nation at Risk* was a politically manipulated and unfounded assault on public education. His argument also supports my claim that many ideological factors are working against public education, most of which have little to do with educating young people in a free and democratic society:

> Conservatives want vouchers and tuition tax credits; liberals want more resources for schools; free marketers want to privatize the schools and make

money; fundamentalists want to teach religion and not worry about the First Amendment; Catholic schools want to stanch their student hemorrhage; home schooling advocates want just that. . . . (p. 621)

And at the center of all of these ideological conflicts noted by Bracey and the complexity of the American psyche we have explored earlier are thousands upon thousands of numbers.

• • •

The 1998 race for governor in SC provides us just one instance of numerical manipulation for political gain; as a natural progression, the debate in SC over education in 2003 also exposes a similar pattern of making ideological leaps of faith cloaked in neat and clear numbers. In 1998, Democrat Jim Hodges, who was bolstered as the favorite of the educational community, ironically gained momentum and a victory in SC by relentlessly bashing educational achievement in the state. The video poker and lottery proponents aided his win by posting billboards throughout the state announcing SC as last in the country in average SAT scores. "Schools need more money and video poker can save our children!" was the political cry, essentially.

As has been typical of such dishonesty, virtually no one raised a voice of opposition, especially not educators who wanted Hodges elected. (Here, we have a real-world example of Bracey's assertion that educators bash education for their gain as well.) And when his Republican opponents did rebuke the claims of Hodges's camp, it was a cry against video gambling (whose lobby supported Hodges), not a challenging of the data about SC education, an education system Republicans bashed as well for being 50th in average SAT scores.

No one with power noted that The College Board itself warns against ranking states by SAT scores since a wide variety of percentages of participation exists from state to state—some with as few as percentages in the single digits, some with over three-quarters of students taking the test. No one with power noted that in SC, more than 50% of seniors take the SAT while only 25% of those students are enrolled in the college preparatory course work recommended by The College Board for anyone attempting the SAT. No one with power noted that SAT scores correlate strongly with socioeconomic status (yet when I did in a local paper, the first to challenge me was a local university's education professor). Few in public education or the public are aware of research that consistently has established socioeconomic status as a key correlation in student performance on standardized tests (Biddle, 1997, pp. 9–13). Yet, SC's school report cards have consistently reflected that schools with high poverty fail while schools with affluence prosper. Just look at all the numbers.

The other side of the educational debate in the state was represented by Republican David Beasley and, to a lesser degree, by a Republican candidate for State Superintendent of Education (both of whom lost primarily because of a push by Democrats to support video poker in the state). They touted higher standards for teachers (including a new testing format that would reward existing teachers with a bonus if they would take the test and that would raise the score needed to gain initial certification); higher standards and a more rigorous, prescriptive curriculum; and choice in education driven by vouchers. Again few knew about or broached the issue that standards raising, often coupled with a Back-to-Basics mantra, had been a regular refrain throughout the 1900s. Nearly no one noted that at any point during this century one could always find those who felt the current state of education was poor and below some romanticized past. For example, the often idealized 1940s and 1950s were punctuated with Bernard Iddings Bell's *Crisis in Education* (1949), Mortimer Smith's *And Madly Teach* (1949), Arthur E. Bestor, Jr.'s *Educational Wastelands* (1953), and eventually Vice Admiral Rickover's criticism of education that led to the late 1950s and early 1960s belief that American education had fallen behind the Soviet system in math and science education, thus the advent of teacher-proof curriculum that is again raising its head today (Kliebard, 1995, pp. 221, 222–223, 226–228). And of course nearly no one pointed to rising evidence that vouchers and other forms of choice do little to raise educational performance either at the schools of choice or at the abandoned schools (Bracey, 1997a, pp. 133–150; Engel, 2000; Pinzur, 2003). And for our purposes, I need to add that throughout all of the debates, statistical data drawn from testing have dominated every camp in every argument—often with opposing camps sharing the same numbers though drawing differing conclusions or supporting contrasting positions, as with Hodges and Beasley in the SC governor's race.

• • •

More recently in 2003, scores from the SAT and from SC's PACT—the hallmark of SC's newest push to comply with NCLB's demands on higher standards for students and schools—have been touted by Governor Mark Sanford and by a local university professor, both through local and state newspaper columns and guest editorials, as clear proof that SC needs school choice. In the state press, Sanford announced that the 2003 PACT scores in English/language arts (ELA) had dropped statewide, thus school choice is the only solution! Concurrent with that pronouncement, a university history professor (who had written Sanford's educational platform during his campaign for governor) in an op-ed piece lamented that SC has continued to languish at the bottom of average state SAT scores and thus we must embrace school choice!

Since numbers don't lie—anyone can see in black and white that the average ELA score on PACT for 2003 is below the 2002 average; anyone can see SC listed at or near the bottom of ranked SAT averages across the nation—those with ideological agendas can easily draw, in the compressed space of media, obvious conclusions and recommend simple solutions. And it works. Playing on the misconceptions and assumptions that dominate American thought, those making these proclamations are virtually never refuted. Briefly, let me highlight some of the dynamics of these two claims above.

First, the SAT and PACT scores may or may not show problems with teaching and learning. Comparing from year-to-year (different populations of students) and state-to-state involves a huge bees nest of statistical problems. In just the PACT score drop in ELA, I am fairly certain that we can draw some useful conclusions about the drop, but not information the politicians want to hear. A body of research is growing that shows our emphasis on standardized testing is actually encouraging ineffective language arts instruction and assessment techniques (Hillocks, 2003; Mabry, 1999; Coles, 2000; Freedman, 1995); thus, in short, raising the standards and increasing the testing have often lowered student achievement, and meaningful learning, in reading and writing. The very nature of being a skilled reader or writer does not lend itself to traditional objective assessment or to reductionistic and fragmented quantifications.

Second, these calls for school choice based on test scores were primarily voiced in the newspapers. In the guest editorial by the professor, the paper printed his piece though it contained several factual errors concerning the SAT. Interesting. More interesting is that at least two letters to the editor noted his errors, but both of the letters' writers were challenged on the factual nature of their letters before the letters were published. Why did the professor's editorial piece slip through the fact-checking mechanism, but the letters did not? Could it be that newspapers often benefit from negative portrayals of schools, but garner little from those who show that maybe schools are often doing a fine job? It's worth considering.

• • •

"It is a well-known adage that what gets measured gets done," claimed SC State Representative Robert W. Harrell Jr. (2003) when he entered the testing debate from the fall of 2003 discussed above. We might counter that weighing a pig doesn't fatten it; simply testing students does not make them smarter, in other words. But Rep. Harrell is not alone in his sentiment and is not unique in his voice of authority on education, regretfully. Hold people accountable or they won't work hard enough; without competition, we lose productivity—these arguments have become the mantras attacking public education.

In his editorial, which followed the comments I noted above about PACT and SAT scores showing a need for school choice, Harrell (2003) made his political stand against a growing issue in the TV media about student test fatigue. A local TV station did a report on test fatigue after the SC State Department of Education noted that the ELA test-score drop correlated with the ELA test being administered last after two weeks of testing. Harrell's response?—"Rather than spending so much time trying to explain away the results, we should be looking for ways to improve our students' language arts skills."

The political dynamic concerning education and the debate unfolding in the media is this: A state representative who is in the insurance business is more expert in his appraisal of educational instruction and assessment than educators themselves. When educators, in fact, question the bureaucracy of implementing educational legislation, those educators are merely being evasive, insincere, lazy. But a politician whose area of expertise is insurance and who ends his editorial with the political and vapid "Their future depends on it" is certainly and expertly only expressing the best of intent toward educating children. Because numbers don't lie.

• • •

To enter the media fray over schools, I submitted this op-ed piece to the *Greenville News* on October 21, 2003:

> Release standardized test scores into the media and politicians gather like sharks in chum-filled water. The analyses that follow are often simplistic and predictable—though lacking in educational merit.
> Recently, there has been much hand wringing over the drop in English/Language Arts (ELA) scores on the Palmetto Achievement Challenge Test (PACT). The governor called for school choice, and the State Depart-

ment of Education blamed test fatigue. The truth is far more complicated—thus far less politically attractive.

Reading and writing are whole activities. When we try to fit literacy performances into standardized testing constraints, the results are disastrous. Driven by the need to be manageable and quantifiable, standardized testing tends to reduce and fragment whole activities into small measurable parts—such as phonemic awareness in reading and grammatical knowledge in writing.

Consider how we would respond if our local football teams practiced all week only to take multiple choice tests each Friday night. Consider how we would respond if our children in art or band never were allowed to create artwork or play an instrument, but they busily labeled the parts of an easel or a French horn each day. Yet, we allow such practices with reading and writing.

Further, we have a tendency to be careless in what we mean by the terms "reading" and "writing." "Reading" in testing situations is often little more than decoding or answering multiple-choice questions on a brief (and often lifeless) passage. In the real world, "reading" is comprehension—and it can be evaluated only by having students both perform extended reading and demonstrate comprehension through whole activities such as discussions or writing.

"Writing" suffers the same dilemma. Standardized tests for decades have passed off mere editing—identifying grammar and usage errors in other people's sentences—as writing. What students need to develop are composing skills. Again this would require having students create their own topics and produce a piece of writing through a lengthy process that cannot be managed or quantified as easily as grammar tests can be.

Robert Coles, a leader in reading research, and George Hillocks, Jr., the foremost national authority on writing instruction, have shown over the past couple decades that as accountability measures and standardized testing expand in both their power and their frequency, reading and writing instruction is negatively impacted; thus, students are being directly harmed in their literacy development by legislation such as No Child Left Behind (NCLB) and South Carolina's own PACT.

In our local schools, the threat of failing school report cards and the looming declaration by the federal government that most schools in SC are failures have forced administrators and teachers to ignore authentic reading and writing instruction in order to address PACT for PACT's sake. Much of our literacy instruction has become isolated to mirror the fragmented nature of standardized tests.

When we reduce reading and writing activities to worksheets that look like PACT, phonics drills, and isolated grammar instruction in order to feed the monsters of NCLB and PACT, we actually harm students' literacy skills and destroy their natural interests as readers and writers. Hillocks, in fact, has shown that direct, isolated grammar instruction produces inferior writing in content and surface features when compared to pieces by students who freely write daily with no teacher input.

Standardizing and standardized tests are by their nature contrary to individual acts such as reading and writing. But neat numbers from high-stakes testing are manageable, and they provide easily manipulated political capital.

The drop in ELA scores on PACT should be a wake-up call. Who do we want dictating how our children learn to read and write? Politicians who have experience in business, insurance, or law? Politicians who may benefit only if they can assure that our schools are labeled failures?

What our children need is both messy and politically neutral. Students need classrooms where teachers are free to engage them in rich reading and writing activities that do not include worksheets, that do not include text books or reading programs, that do not include checklists of curriculum to cover passed down from Washington, DC, or Columbia.

Reading and writing instruction are the most valuable gifts we can give our students; language is their passport to empowered lives. The current drop in ELA scores on PACT is an indictment—but not on our children or our teachers. It is an indictment on our political leaders who are enjoying a season of playing political football with the education of children.

And such is the mix; politicians, lay people, educators, and parents take big swings at this thing called public education. As Bracey (2003b) argues in his aptly titled book, *On the Death of Childhood and the Destruction of Public Schools*, we find ourselves wrestling and gaining few positive accomplishments.

• • •

The education debate is pregnant with political dishonesty, but often nested within political dishonesty is philosophical dishonesty, or at least philosophical bias couched in objective rhetoric; and there is where the media becomes a key player in the unfounded assault on schools (See Bracey, 2003b, for another discussion of the media's role). While all societies, all countries, have their culture wars, America is currently in the throes of a right wing versus left wing war that is at least intense, if not unique. That struggle is being played out in the defining glare of the media, from 24-hour TV news networks to radio talk shows. Education is never too long absent from those arguments. In that larger arena, we see philosophical dishonesty; it is currently vogue to trash liberal media as biased while praising right-wing media as "the truth," or as a "no-spin zone"—to use the euphemisms of dishonesty by two of the more popular figures in right-wing media.

• • •

Again a glance at the development of 20th-century American education shows a steady struggle for the philosophical control of schools, which is also a struggle for control of the intellectual capital in this country (Kliebard, 1995; Watras, 2004). As mentioned earlier, conveniently packaged as an endorsement of a surprisingly effective curriculum program, Nicholas Lemann's "'Ready Read!'" (published in the *Atlantic*) actually serves as one, though not unique, example of ideology clothed as expertise. The philosophical bias by Lemann is shown in a few of his points, dropped in rather quickly and passed off as facts, not his opinion, and as clearly desirable outcomes:

> Success for All tells schools precisely what to teach and how to teach it—to the point of scripting, nearly minute by minute, every teacher's activity in every classroom every day of the year. . . . [T]he key [to the success of P.S. 144] was the imposition of a tightly defined, proven reading curriculum. . . . Success for All turns teachers into drill instructors. The atmosphere is palpably one of preparing children to become workers. . . . By far the best and most reliable means for turning these schools around would be to institute a prescribed curriculum that has been carefully researched and field-tested and has been proved to work. (Lemann, 1998, pp. 98, 102, 104)

Lemann clearly embraces a belief in empirical data (the truth in numbers), a belief that schools should produce workers (again, see Bracey, 2003b, and Ayers, 2001, for arguments against that view), and a belief that teachers should get out of the way of a content-rich prescribed curriculum. Such ideas manifest themselves in the media and thus carry a certain weight since they are published in some way and since that publishing carries power in the American mind. While such is the nature of discourse in many ways, the cloaked nature of the influence placed on society needs to be addressed.

The hybrid dishonesty that is upon us now can be seen in Lemann's piece (though I offer this as just one example of a common practice, a practice often performed by good people with good intentions side by side with those of lesser character and with less credible motives). More and more politicians and pundits have realized that if an objective, standardized test is designed first, and if that test dictates a prescribed curriculum that can be scripted and easily quantified and displayed, and if teachers can be forced to train students along that and only that curricular course, tests scores will increase, the public will be pleased (though horribly fooled), and the careers of politicians and pundits will have been boosted. (Consider the career boost afforded Rod Paige after such occurred in Texas.) In addition, if data continues to show public schools as failures, then vouchers along with other forms of school choice can be swept in with little complaint. Of course nowhere is there any real concern for educating students in this process. And that is where we are, unless educators lead

the charge for a new educational honesty. Informed practitioners in
education must begin to speak louder than numbers.

• • •

Some educators have begun to swim against the building river of
educational dishonesty. But the current is strong. Regie Routman
(1996) offers an effective example of how to raise the educational discourse to a more honest level, how to reject the simplistic force of
numbers and explore the complexity of educational issues. Routman's
work presents a much more complex, a more sincerely research-based
and historically accurate argument for addressing reading concerns
than is common in the mainstream media. As we compare Routman's
agenda, educational, with Lemann's assumptions, empirical and po-
litical/ideological, we can see the profound impact numbers play on
the American public at large. Remember that ultimately numbers
don't lie; people do, even when they believe themselves to be sincere
and factual.

Routman (1996) confronts the backlash against whole language
reading instruction. Realizing that much of the information on education presented to the public is expressed by people who are not
educators, she mentions journalists (as have others, notably Watson,
1998), but increasingly, the public receives information about education through politicians with the aid of the media and often neatly
packaged with an imposing display of numbers and charts. Such was
the case when California was held up to America as a state that had
chosen whole language, had failed students during 10 years of whole
language, and had finally abandoned whole language. Routman,
however, points out that many factors contributed to California's
troublesome reading scores over a decade—increased class size, lowering of educational funding, ill-equipped schools and libraries, an
increase in non-English speaking students, a lack of staff development for implementing whole language (pp. 18–33). It seems that
when *all* the numbers are explored, not simply selected numbers that
support an agenda, the conclusions about educational issues are
much more complex and politically less attractive.

Further, Routman (1996) discovered that in most cases, of the
schools that claimed to be implementing whole language, only 20% of
its reading faculty actually understood whole language. How many
actually *implemented* whole language in the classroom remains un-
known, though we can say with certainty that most students received
traditional reading instruction during the so-called failure in Califor-

nia (p. 36). (In WWII, the same scenario occurred; soldiers proved to be semiliterate or illiterate at surprisingly high numbers. The common cry was to blame progressive, Deweyan education, but virtually all of those soldiers had attended traditional schools.) Equally important is that in the not-too-distant past, reading scores were lamented during the heyday of isolated and direct phonics instruction as well, thus the call for a new methodology that has led to a claimed, but unfulfilled, commitment to whole language.

Further, the whole language movement has coincided with the increased concern for standardized testing; since whole language is best assessed through authentic measures (students *creating* responses, not *selecting* responses), standardized test scores often do not accurately reflect what students have learned in a whole-language setting. Change the format of the assessment, change what students do, and the numbers representing achievement for the same student will change, though the level of understanding in the student will not. (For instance, a young boy who has collected baseball cards his whole life, who has lived baseball stats, might appear genius on a multiple-choice test on baseball trivia, though he may fail miserably at a baseball tryout; the boy is the same boy, though the assessment expectations change.) Routman (1996) laments that standardized tests emphasize students' weaknesses, not their achievement; schools have consistently increased the time spent teaching test-taking reading (how to answer objective multiple-choice questions on a brief selection), not authentic reading.

As a brief aside, consider the power that the test has over our conception of learning. If we design a standardized test that measures phonemic awareness through a series of isolated, multiple-choice (selected-response) questions, the test decision clearly affects outcomes. Students drilled in isolated phonics instruction would certainly score higher on that test than students who have been in holistic and authentic classrooms where they speak, write, and read. Conversely, if we place students from that same instructional setting of direct isolated phonics instruction in a testing situation where they have to perform authentically (create responses), then their scores would be vastly different than on the multiple-choice test, such as with the baseball example above. The children didn't change, but the testing showed them to be different. The assumptions and manageability of our tests are dictating what we call learning, and are dictating what matters in our disciplines.

In short, Routman (1996) identifies the enormous complexity that educational issues present. No one scapegoat exists; no one cure exists. Actually, education has shown steady improvement over the years (Bracey, 1997a; Moore & Simon, 2000). But we still have much to improve; we will always have much to improve. Education can and should be improved. That improvement will depend heavily, however, on educators taking the initiative to address education honestly. But, of course, all of that is complicated mightily by the popular and political power invested in the numbers we gather on our students.

• • •

The whole language debate in California in the late 1980s and early 1990s has also been addressed by Stephen Krashen (2002b) who places the situation in a context relevant here: Cultural assumptions blend with political and ideological manipulations to create a powerful phenomenon known as "urban legends." By using the same numbers as Routman and those who were politically and financially motivated (phonics-based commercial programs or games and textbook companies, for instance) to denounce whole language reading instruction, Krashen explores the political fallout of reading instruction in California; additionally, he was directly involved with the California Language Arts Framework Committee, thus offering direct information on the actual mandates and actual practices concerning reading in the state.

Krashen (2002b; 2003) shows not only that the failure of whole language was an urban legend in California, but also that NCLB is a similar manipulation of data to promote a political/ideological agenda. Joanne Yatvin (2002) has the same insider knowledge as Krashen, except that she was originally involved in the National Reading Panel (NRP) that fed NCLB legislation; Yatvin also shows that the NRP was not a scientific process of discovering the best reading instruction strategies as shown by decades of research, but was a politically driven body designed to fulfill a predetermined end—endorse isolated, phonics-based reading programs that are easily prescribed and easily quantified in standardized testing. In other words, politicians are offering ample evidence that they use numbers to grow political capital in the public schools.

• • •

While educators and researchers such as Routman, Krashen, and Bracey slip their voices into the mix, the loudest voices continue to be self-appointed education experts who have disproportionate access to the mass media. Again, another example of such an inexpert voice is Walter Williams in a piece from October 26, 2003; his "The Key to Education? No Excuses" typifies the public debate in the snapshot of editorial opinions: "The route to greater academic excellence is nearly a no-brainer," Williams proclaims.

In a condescending voice—how could educators be so stupid (and probably lazy!)—Williams (2003) echoes the mantra that runs through the right-wing assault on schools: The solutions are easy and obvious; the solutions cost no money; too many teachers are "incompetent [and] uncaring"; test data, here NAEP, clearly support all of these points. The media's nature, that information is condensed and preferably provocative, helps contribute to simplistic and inflammatory commentary. Williams is far from alone in this carelessness, and if such voices weren't so loud, if the experts in the field of education had at least an equally powered megaphone, then the situation wouldn't be so dire. But the truth is that the most powerful voices in the debate over the running of our schools and in the judging of our schools and teachers are those who have little or no training or experience as teachers. All they have are numbers and ideology.

After my guest editorial included earlier, I exchanged a series of e-mails with a person (a name was never offered) who relentlessly defended standardized testing and directly stated that anyone who is "educated" is also qualified to educate others. This societal lack of respect and even disdain for professional educators runs throughout the success of those who manipulate the public with political and philosophical dishonesty, who see the school debate as solid footing to other goals.

• • •

Educators must acknowledge that we are increasingly overwhelming students, primarily because too many factions contribute to the educational mix—parents through school boards, politicians through legislation, publishers through textbooks, journalists through the media, and educators as practitioners. Prescribed curriculum guides, statewide standards, high-stakes testing, and textbooks often create a monster too large for either teachers or students to handle.

American texts suffer several problems that must be addressed, counter-educational impacts that are magnified during this era of raising standards and increased measurement. First, texts often serve as *the* curriculum for many teachers regardless of district or state mandates, regardless of the authority within the field, regardless of the teacher's own expertise; texts must become instead supplements to instruction in American classrooms, not the curriculum. Also texts are increasingly huge, bland, and boring—and just plain inaccurate, often by omission (Daniels & Zemelman, 2003/2004). Parents and quasi-political groups have gained more and more control over text adoptions (Raymo, 1998); therefore, many textbook publishers, wanting sales above all else (profit is a number that impacts education as well), excise anything potentially controversial from many texts, leaving us with books that are often intellectually uninteresting at best and inaccurate at worst. The result is students plowing through oversimplified secondary sources throughout their schooling without ever working through primary sources and reaching conclusions themselves.

Additionally, texts in America are far too big and contain far too much pure information. Dempster (1993) states, "Unfortunately, many texts are so packed with facts, names, and details that the real point of the lesson is often obscured" (p. 434). He has noted that our texts cover considerably more content in math and science than many other industrialized countries, ones often touted as superior to us on standardized tests—though that *coverage* mentality (ever increasing under federal and state pushes for high standards) excludes the far more significant conceptual understanding that students will find valuable in the real world. The American lust for quantity over quality is clearly reflected in our textbook mania and its contribution to coverage over understanding.

This textbook phenomenon is lamented directly by writer Barbara Kingsolver (2002) when she recognizes that weak science texts are at least somewhat accountable for weak scientific understanding in American culture. When discussing the essential lack of understanding concerning Darwin and basic evolutionary theory (or even a basic understanding of the "theory"), Kingsolver offers: "I blame the religious fanatics who kept basic biology out of [students'] grade-school textbooks" (p. 102). She is well aware that the simplistic American psyche is quick to discount any challenging idea as "just a theory" because most are "ignorant of what that word means" (p. 96). Where ideology and knowledge intersect is the fight over texts—a fight that is currently broiling, although both sides experience victories (Gillespie, 2003; Harmon, 2003; Krauss & Princehouse, 2003). Raymo (1998) adds that the careless attitude in America about facts and theories grows from inappropriate influences on what goes into texts:

Our school-kids do not need intellectual security blankets. By insisting that science textbooks be warm and fuzzy, fundamentalists encourage the infantilization of the next generation of Americans. (p. 144)

Within the NCLB tidal wave is another serious textbook issue: The not-so-subtle endorsing of Open Court (McGraw-Hill) as *the* reading program for any district wishing to retain its federal funding (though the percentage of funds any state receives in the U.S. is often no more than 8%). Coles (2003) and Yatvin (2002) have demonstrated that the numbers used by both the NRP and McGraw-Hill are distorted at best and unethical at worst. The touted research behind Open Court is of essentially no merit since "[a]ll one finds there is 'research' done under the aegis of the publisher" (Coles, 2003). Apparently America learned nothing from the tobacco industry and its own scientific data on smoking.

Textbook issues are also money issues, that ever-lurking number in America. With NCLB, schools and states risk losing federal funding if the *right* reading programs are not adopted (Goodnough, 2003). Horvitz (2003) also identifies the potential boom for publishers who comply with NCLB—"it could mean up to $6 billion in sales during the next six years for education [textbook] companies." That profit number raises its head once again.

• • •

Another area for educators to attack vigorously and honestly is the standardized test, the leading source of numbers games in our country. The SAT has gained unprecedented importance in America not only as an indicator of individual student intelligence, but also as a measure of the success of school districts and entire states. This public perception has occurred despite the SAT being only the third or fourth best predictor of student success in college, the purpose for which the test was designed. GPA, the level of difficulty of courses taken, and, perhaps, well-roundedness of the student are better predictors of college success than is the SAT (Jenkins, 1992; Fincher, 1990; Baron & Norman, 1992). As well, the SAT has reached its lofty status as an indicator of statewide educational success despite The College Board's instructions that SAT scores should never be used to rank and compare states.

Educators are now faced with explaining to the general public exactly what each standardized test is designed to do. Then we must begin an honest but determined campaign to lobby for a transition away from our dependency on students bubbling in answers they merely choose to tests that require students to generate responses. Ongoing authentic assessment as a part of instruction is the primary role assessment must play in improving student achievement, and that approach to assessment must trump the current misguided trust we put in assessment that is quick and easily quantifiable. Rarely do educators practice authentic assessment; even more rare is anyone's questioning the faith we place in standardized testing. Yes, bubbled answer sheets are quicker to grade, cheaper to grade, and (possibly) more objective and reliable. But we must be honest about the authenticity of assessment. Multiple-choice testing will never assess as validly for improved instruction and learning as will authentic measures. No one would let a school determine the state championship in football based on abstract multiple-choice testing on a cold Friday night in November each year (Childress, 1998). We have always known that athletes, as well as musicians and artists, must perform, create their own authentic displays of their abilities. Every student in every classroom in America deserves no less. We seem to know at some level that the numbers displayed after a football game carry the weight they do because *the game was played.*

• • •

As we reeducate educators and the public about testing, we must also reeducate society about the nature of education, specifically in three areas—education versus training, the complexity and current status of education, and the primary importance of reading instruction at the early grades. Just as Lemann's article on reading and Kliebard's discussion of the history of curriculum debate show, Americans have fought for at least a century over what education is and, perhaps, more importantly, should be; all the while numbers have been at the center of those fights. Many seem to endorse rote memorization and strict training of young people, which commonly passes as education in closed societies. Educators must fight against all such attempts at indoctrination in the name of education. As Thomas Jefferson saw it, education is the essential element in a democracy. Free people can run a republic only as well as they are educated—educated in the sense that they have personal and communal awareness and are reflective, knowledgeable thinkers. Albert Einstein urged,

> If [schools] are able to teach young people to have a critical mind and a socially oriented attitude, they will have done all that is necessary. Students will then become equipped with those qualities which are prerequisite for

citizens living in a healthy democratic society. (*Essential Einstein*, 6 November 1998)

I would argue that we will never find a suitable way to quantify with any accuracy "a critical mind" or "a socially oriented attitude," but I am quite certain those are qualities our schools need to foster in our children.

Yet education that is not indoctrination—education that guides students as they interact with information, a wide variety of information and perspectives on that information, and that responds to those students as they produce authentic responses—is highly complex and often chaotic. America, despite our claim to individuality, includes a large majority of people who accept linear thinking and regimented thought as the norm, even as the desired pinnacle of what we want from educated children. Thus we as educators must reeducate the public to both the complexity of education and the undeniable fact that American education is the best it has ever been, even though we will need to stoop to legitimate numbers to help make our claims (Moore & Simon, 2000), and that public education is *not* the inferior cousin of private schools (Benveniste, Carnoy, & Rothstein, 2003).

Stating that public education today is the best it has ever been is not enough, however. We must assert honestly that education is still not good enough; it never will be. Working from the premise that we have an essentially flawed (as the Right wishes to claim) and regressive system is drastically different from the premise that we are at our best but the envelope must be pushed. American education must move toward *kaizen*, continuous, incremental improvement (Owens, 1995, p. 20). For Americans, we need to look no further than Chuck Yeager, who epitomized pushing the envelope as a pilot, though he was carelessly tossed aside as America moved into the Space Age (Yeager and other such pilots somehow were not the material NASA desired, though they personified the idealized spirit of adventure many associate with America). Yeager, like Einstein and others, combined intuition and logic while pursuing his goal and his dreams. American education must begin to function on a course that constantly moves forward without razing all that has come before, including maintaining some of our need to quantify.

• • •

Concurrent with reorienting America's thinking about education in the abstract, educators must face one certainty: Literacy must be the essential focus of the primary and elementary years of education.

The facts and content knowledge from our first 4 or 5 years of schooling certainly mean little in the long run; and even if those facts do matter, facts are easier to gain later in schooling than essential *acts*, such as independent, productive reading and writing ability. Students leaving third or fourth grade as independent and *willing* readers and writers will benefit more from their educational experience than our current focus on third graders taking a wide range of standardized tests that do not force the students to produce anything, except merely to bubble, except merely to meet the score. Constantly *measuring* literacy ability is not fostering literacy.

● ● ●

Finally, we must focus a sincere effort in the classroom to be honest with students about our content areas. My daughter, as early as fourth grade, had already suffered enough falsehoods and distortions driven by rarely acknowledged ideological intent to confuse her and disillusion her for a lifetime. In those 5 years she has been led to believe Helen Keller was a conventional woman (with the implication being that she was a *good, patriotic American*—a true conformist to all that is good and American), not the radical-thinking socialist she was; she has been told not to start sentences with "and" or "but," that fragments are wrong, despite professional writers doing all of those and suffering no negative consequences; she has been convinced that social studies and English are boring, nothing except a set of mindless vocabulary she is not yet able to comprehend, as a result of mind-numbing texts and a curriculum designed to increase test scores.

Constance Weaver (1996) has stated, for example, that in English classes we should not hold students to artificial standards that professionals routinely ignore. Such is the kind of content honesty we need to pursue. Helen Keller was not a conventional American, and professional writers often use fragments. Which on occasion can be effective. Clinging to that which is easily transferred to the student, that which is most manageable to assess and quantify, and that which fulfills jingoistic propaganda is the most morally and educationally bankrupt behavior existing in education. If we begin to be honest with our students we can help foster an American society that will see the value in the type of education needed for American democracy to thrive. The ugly complicated truth—it cannot be measured or reduced to a number—must be at the center of all that we teach.

Nothing is as simple as we would like it to be. Education and our approaches to teaching certainly are not simple. Yet we do know what to do. We have known it at least since John Dewey began considering the big issues of teaching and learning as this century began. One of the keys that will start the move toward a *better* educational system in America is honesty and leadership from educators themselves. In an era in which empty platitudes and huge displays of testing data often clash with bitter cynicism, it appears that "honesty is the best policy" might be our best bet, honestly.

Political Agendas and Public Schools— It Came from the 1980s

Upon the twentieth anniversary of the educational report possibly with the greatest public scrutiny ever in education, Bracey (2003a) opens his discussion of *A Nation at Risk* by describing a political wrestling match between James Baker and Ed Meese in the Reagan White House. Bracey understands that education is more often than not a pawn in a bigger political game. That educational initiative also had its numbers components—"more science, more mathematics, . . . more time on task, more hours in the school day, more days in the school year. . ." (p. 617). Measurement was the key to everything in the Reagan plan for schools, yet the ultimate agenda had far more to do with ideology and social engineering than it did with education.

A Nation at Risk, now 20 years in our past, represents the logical penultimate political assault on education before NCLB. As well, that report under Reagan now clearly reveals the mix—politics, the media, numbers and measurement, and a gullible American public—that threatens the potential our schools hold but are unable to pursue. Bracey (2003a) characterizes the Reagan report as "a veritable treasury of slanted, spun, and distorted statistics" (p. 617). Now that many years of living with and examining *A Nation at Risk* and the ideas and numbers behind it have passed, we can see more clearly Bracey's assertion that "no actual *data* [supported] the contention that high test scores implied competitiveness," or any of the other conclusions and mandates (both stated and implied) in this political document (p. 619). Bracey echoes Peter Applebome's final declaration on the report—"propaganda" (p. 620).

While Yatvin (2003) has offered one insider's voice in the refuting of George W. Bush's equally propagandistic NCLB, her voice has remained fairly muted. Gerald Holton (2003) has joined Yatvin in spirit by offering his own insider's analysis drawn from his direct involvement with *A Nation at Risk*. Holton's discussion contributes to my discussion here on the key dynamics involved in political answers to educational problems: what politicians *want*, often cloaked in a call for improving schools, raising standards, and serving the children of America and its democratic soul; what research and the reports that follow actually say; what journalists and other pundits pronounce based on those reports, that research, and how the politicians react themselves; and what the public sees and hears, despite what is actually said or displayed in print or via a vast array of media. With the clarity of hindsight, we can see through *A Nation at Risk* and watch these dynamics in action.

Holton (2003) speaks about his experience in the context of NCLB: "The disjunction between rhetoric and reality [today] has an uncanny resemblance to the situation two decades ago." The political agendas of Reagan and Bush have found a neat comfort in masking their agendas in the rhetoric of numbers. For that masking to work, Reagan's committee, as noted by Holton, had "not one prominent national expert on education," though Holton himself names many who would have served well to speak on the condition of schools in America. Further, Holton witnessed himself the decree made by Reagan officials about the charge of the commission on education:

> Bring God back into the classroom. Encourage tuition tax credits for families using private schools. Support vouchers. Leave the primary responsibility for education to parents. And please abolish that abomination, the Department of Education.

That agenda includes a great deal of capitalistic intent and social engineering, and a good dose of politics, but it seems to have little to do with education and a great deal to do with the inherent blind spots I have outlined in the American psyche so far. Holton and others on the commission grew nervous from the start.

When the commission did its work and began to make recommendations and write the report, the mix grew even more inept. Holton (2003) describes conclusions that were contrary to what the Reagan administration desired, but those conclusions sound eerily like the situation we are facing today in the NCLB-driven school reform. Some of the conclusions relevant to this discussion are "more rigorous, measurable standards" and accountability, most notably.

So, *A Nation at Risk* built a solid base for Bush's NCLB in terms of measurable standards, testing, and accountability, along with the use of educational initiatives for political gains. As well, Holton (2003) reminds us that "an unbelievable flood of publicity [followed] the report." Yes, the media played a prominent hand in the cry that the sky was falling in our schools, both in the 1980s and today. While "Reagan used 'A Nation at Risk' as a Trojan horse to help win the election," according to Holton, many in mainstream America jumped into the fray about our schools, including the National Academy of Sciences (certainly its title alone struck many Americans with awe), journalists and pundits, and conflicting voices of educators big and small.

Even Holton's valuable response to his experience with and analysis of *A Nation at Risk* should give us pause today. While he proclaims the need to protect public education in the name of democracy, his analysis and recommendations are sprinkled with the exact assumptions that I believe make saving our public schools nearly impossible; he calls for a need to professionalize teaching (yet many state governments have manipulated that already through National Board Certification, numbers in the form of teacher pay), a need to reexamine the content of courses (yet a focus on content only exacerbates the potential to produce and validate the worst of standardized testing and prescribed curriculums), and a need to "tie tests more closely to the curriculum" (just say no to teaching to the test, please). Holton (2003) speaks with great conviction about public education, democracy, and the frailty of the disenfranchised, specifically children, but his own words leave too much room for further assaults on all those things with numbers drawn from testing, testing, and more testing.

And the media joins Holton and others in revisiting *A Nation at Risk* with an eye solidly on NCLB. Lynn Olson (2003b), for instance, covers in *Education Week* the growing consensus in America that educational reform under Reagan, though huge and unprecedented at the time, has "failed to confront 'essential issues of power and control' in U.S. schools." It may give us momentary hope to see that many are declaring a defining political solution to educational reform a failure; could a rejection of the methods—testing, data collecting, and the like—be far behind? I doubt it. Olson's reporting turns immediately to the critics of *A Nation at Risk* and their solutions: "Every school . . . should be held to rigorous, statewide academic standards; statewide assessments of students and school performance; and statewide systems of incentives and interventions tied to academic results." Hmm. Did anyone read *A Nation at Risk*? The solutions are the same again and again, as if the report or the program (*A Nation at Risk* or NCLB) is the problem and not the approaches themselves, not how the solutions look *in the classrooms*. We might take a cue from politicians at the point and begin to shout, "It's the numbers, stupid!"

Not all the voices being raised in this debate fail to see that plowing the same ground is futile. Schmoker (2003) reports that a few are beginning to recognize that the *process* itself is failing schools. As long as we maintain a system of top-down mandates that require institution planning involving goals, action plans, and the like—all tied to a staggering array of measurements because we must hold those spending our tax dollars accountable—we are destined to fail. "Superficially, [strategic plans] are large, handsome documents; school boards, district offices, and accreditation agencies love them," Schmoker concludes. Maybe, "It's the strategic planning, stupid!"

Profits and Prophets of Doom—
Textbooks and Reading Programs

The so-called failed reform under Reagan that swelled over the past two decades has culminated in today's NCLB; while I will always argue this is nothing new, I also concede that it is at least unique. We have looked briefly at the role textbooks have played in hurting students since texts are often corrupted by a variety of influences that ultimately censor the best any field of study has to offer and by an American commitment that more is better. In the context of the evolution of political solutions to education from Reagan through George W. Bush, we can also see that politicians have seen their failures as well and have learned lessons, troubling lessons that include scientific research, textbooks, and reading programs.

A diverse crowd has pointed a critical finger at textbooks; note Barbara Kingsolver's anger earlier in this chapter. Holton (2003) also detailed that the *A Nation at Risk* commission found that "[t]extbooks had become unchallenging and repetitious." Two phenomena are at play here (again with numbers, measurements, and political ideology not too far in the background): The lesson learned by politicians concerning programs and textbooks (control the programs with federal funds and you run the classrooms) and the grassroots political power of textbook adoption processes across the U.S.

In "The Federal Hickory Stick for Teaching Reading," Coles (2003) masterfully characterizes the lesson learned from Reagan's failures: "The Bush administration has had no trouble reversing its purported antipathy toward big government and establishing, through the lure of federal funds, a nationally mandated reading curriculum." Someone is trying to be reelected, and someone is about to get rich quick on textbook adoptions. At the center of this move under NCLB is the term "science," again. Coles, and many others, explains that McGraw-Hill's Open Court reading program is supported by the publisher's own research—a no-no in any branch of the sciences and respectable research—and that Open Court is merely a fulfillment of the Bush mandate, not a solution to reading problems in our students. Experts such as Coles in the field of reading recognize the dynamic, but so far, the lure of phonics continues to work with the American public, so easily led by the words "science" and "research."

And the hickory stick breaks backs. New York City had been standing firm in its choice of reading programs, one that is balanced in its approaches to reading instruction (in other words, one that is grounded in whole language), but the lure of "$34 million was too much money to give up" (Herszenhorn, 2004). This concession for federal money at the expense of the welfare of children reveals the political pull of NCLB tied to key words, such as "scientific," and cold hard cash.

While the Bush administration has learned to mandate educational policy and even classroom practice through "scientifically based" standards under federal legislation (the Reading First criteria of NCLB) and to indirectly endorse commercial reading programs (McGraw-Hill's Open Court, for example) by connecting federal dollars to guidelines for required reading programs, those with ideological agendas learned quite some time ago that schools can be shaped close to home by entering the textbook adoption process. Special interest groups (Schafersman, 2003) and the media (Manzo, 2002) have taken note of the growing influence textbooks and the textbook adoption process have over our schools. Added to that is the financial gain waiting at the end of that process (Horvitz, 2003). If we care about children and learning, these numbers are frightening.

The textbook adoption process is a microcosm of the phenomenon I have explored so far—a mix of politics, scientific research (numbers), profit, and a naïve or misguided American public. The Center for Education Reform (CER) identifies three essential facts about how texts get into our children's hands:

- At least 20 states have highly centralized and bureaucratic control of textbook adoption that is manipulated by state funding.

- California, Texas, and Florida virtually control the textbook market for the entire country.

- McGraw-Hill (recall Open Court?), Houghton Mifflin, Harcourt, and Pearson dominate "70 percent of the industry." ("The Textbook Conundrum," 2001; "Textbook Adoption Needs Second Look," 2001)

Funding, ideology, concentrated power, and special interest groups add up to a dangerous formula for our students.

The same report ("The Textbook Conundrum," 2001) notes that since the textbooks often become the curriculum, the impact of text adoption is huge, even in the face of high standards and testing for accountability. "Teachers and parents seem to think that if it's in the books, it must be the way our kids should learn," the CER's report concludes. Echoing Holton (2003), this report quotes A. Graham Down: "[T]he current system of textbook adoption has filled our schools with Trojan horses—glossily covered blocks of paper whose words emerge to deaden the minds of our nation's youth, and make them enemies of learning." Down shares Kingsolver's and Raymo's anger over bad texts and the bad learning they create. Ambitious text publishers with enough resources, however, scramble to reflect those standards and tests in their textbooks and the ancillary materials they provide in order to grab their market share quickly. The result is that educators and even parents are left out of the loop—though bureaucrats, profiteers, and vocal special interest groups have open access to this process.

In the 1980s when the Religious Right began to infiltrate school boards and raise a cry against textbooks, it almost seemed quaint. That grassroots movement, though, has mushroomed into a federal hickory stick that costs and generates millions upon millions of dollars and immeasurable (ironically) political capital for those who wield power. Are our reading, math, and science texts weak? I think so. But it may be the numbers and the gnashing of teeth that stand behind how they get into the classroom that should concern us most since federal legislation and funding have closed the book on any debate for now.

NCLB has produced little that is solid in terms of educating children and leaving no child behind. But it has created one phenomenon that is at least disturbing: "Companies that sell to the schools—from test publishers to tutoring services to teacher-training outfits—say business is booming" (Kronholz, 2003). Yes, money is to be made through our schools, and those numbers should make us pause when "[t]est publishers are the most obvious winners" in an educational initiative mandated by the federal government.

Blind-sided from the Right— Print Media, Science, Numbers, and Schools

This chapter begins with a look at the media's role in this wrestling match with our schools. As I work toward the chapter's end, I want to readdress journalists at the center of the educational debate, since they have a loud voice in the conversation, one that is heavily tainted with ideology and their own misconceptions about science, numbers, and education.

Journalists who are commentators—they write editorials for the print media or offer commentary on TV or host talk-show formats on the radio—often weave social and ideological mind-sets throughout their work despite their topics. In the last 2 decades such commentary has become dominated by a conservative slant, oddly as a response to the so-called biased liberal media. As I noted earlier, common in that conservative voice is a proclamation that the right-wing viewpoint is the truth, that a conservative opinion is unbiased. For this discussion, we'll stop with making that observation; no need to highlight the faults with those stances here.

As we explore education and numbers, we are most concerned with the dynamic and the elements within that dynamic, and I hope raising our awareness of the dynamic will aid in addressing any changes needed to improve our schools. Maggie Gallagher, a syndicated columnist, offers two columns only a couple months apart in 2003 that show the impact of her ideology, particularly her conservative view of society, and her assumptions about science and education on her voice in the educational debate (I would argue, her unfairly loud voice).

Science *proves* my social agenda: Gallagher (2003b) holds a fairly typical conservative stance that the sky is falling in terms of social moral decline. She writes in one piece about a scientific study that proves her belief that eroding social morality is destroying our children: "The larger message of this scientific report is that American society is failing children and teenagers." As I mentioned in Chapter One, I doubt that many right-wing commentators grab science so quickly when it proves evolution in the form of natural selection being as much a fact as gravity. But social pundits like politicians have learned recently to embrace science when it suits their needs; that is a drastic shift from just a few decades ago when the Religious Right distanced itself from science at all costs. We have come a long way in some aspects since the Scopes trial of the 1920s. When a study seems to support a conservative view that society is in moral decline *because* of the left—feminists, the popular media (movies and music, remember Elvis?), nontraditional homes—then that study is gospel.

As with the average person, Gallagher and most in the media who draw conclusions from research, whether it be the SAT or moral erosion, make two key mistakes. First, media responses to research studies, *single* studies, often place far too much emphasis on one study. Anyone who conducts research knows that we are looking for *bodies* of research, we are looking for patterns and trends to hang our hats on if those studies stand up to persistent peer review. One study might be interesting, might deserve a spotlight, might raise questions, but it does not *prove* anything, even if its conclusions jibe with our ideology. Also common with pundit proclamations about research is confusing correlation with causation. When you spend enough time with research, you find that correlations are easy to come by, but determining causation is close to impossible. In the mind of most people not familiar with research, the exact opposite assumption is made; causation is easy to proclaim.

One study is conducted and the rallying cry becomes, "Out with public education and teacher certification!" The recent assault on public education is a much more intense attack on the certification of teachers. Oddly, as the federal government and the Right have begun to call for higher qualifications for teachers, they have simultaneously discredited schools of education and courses in education. All that one needs to teach, they claim, is content knowledge. Gallagher (2003a) enters that debate with a claim that one study, again, proves that charter schools' successes show the failures of both public education and the certifying of teachers. She begins her questioning of teacher certification, again based on one study of the relative success of charter schools as compared to traditional public schools, by asserting her credentials for discussing education: "I should know [what makes a good teacher]. I am married to one." Here, Gallagher shows the most common flaw with those in the media who make commentaries on education: The most remote connection anyone has with education makes that person qualified to speak about education. I equate this attitude with a similar idea—having flown on a plane makes one qualified to pilot one. Or maybe not.

Journalists and pundits aren't bad people, at least most surely are not, but they have instant access to speaking at large. The very nature of their profession gives them authority, and the public is quite gullible to that power of voice. Like the general public, journalists are victims of false and simplistic views of science. One study can carry the weight of proof (correlation equals causation); they are blinded by their own ideological lenses (society is in moral decline); and are gravely mistaken that virtually anything makes one qualified to hold court concerning education (such as, "I'm married to a teacher").

Talking Numbers—Approaching the Truth

Traditionally, the running of schools has been left substantially to local control—local school boards, state boards of education, and state government. While NCLB ironically threatens that, coming as it does from Republicans who champion local control and often characterize Big Government as evil, the voices attacking our schools tend to come loud and direct from local conservative talk radio. Control of our schools may be drifting toward centralized federal control, but criticism of our schools still plays out often in the local media.

Let's return to the same talk-show host with whom I begin this chapter. Again, he has claimed education as his area of expertise (despite having no training or experience as an educator), and the newest promo for his afternoon slot is a clip where he flatly states that schools aren't underfunded; he claims schools are *over*funded. He also maintains that no teacher shortage exists, that student-teacher ratios don't matter, and that if he were given control of schools he could solve all the problems with one solution, competition.

His talk-radio show rarely strays too far from issues concerning education, and he routinely attacks the local school district as well as public education as an institution. Public education is essentially flawed, he argues, since it is a socialistic enterprise, outside the glorious competition model that he and his ilk believe to be faultless. While he and many commentators on education are trapped in their ideology and their pursuit of simple answers to complex problems, his discussions are always sprinkled with research. Much like Gallagher, he enjoys touting the isolated study that conforms to his views (though you best not call in with contradictory bodies of research, unless you want to be called over the airwaves a liberal and an educrat). But I don't entirely blame him since such is the nature of American media, conducive as it is to sound bites that come quick and hard and leave little time to distinguish among the kinds of information offered; many talk-radio hosts are adept at mixing seamless opinions with facts so that they all become of the same gravity.

Talk radio loves to bash public education since it is the most visible and largest aspect of the American landscape that is blatant socialism. If public schools succeed can communism be far behind?—they seem to fear. Rarely is the socialistic nature of the military, the police force, or our highway system ever challenged, though. Somehow those valued institutions get a free pass, probably because there is no perception that the socialism in those systems might *influence* the minds of children; soldiers are indoctrinated, of course, but it is *our* party line they are fed, so all is well. Good capitalistic children cannot possibly come out of a socialistic system (though for a century, they *have*).

I have no delusion that we in education are without bias, without our ideologies, without our own manipulations of data. Educators have been equally guilty (and I would say more culpable because we should have known better) of data manipulation. If educators ever admitted that public education *was* successful, then they feared funds would be cut; the best way to keep the money flowing is to bemoan teacher pay, student-teacher ratios, lack of technology, and such. While some of these complaints have valid kernels of truth, educators have essentially lied as well, especially when numbers served our purposes and especially when the media lent a sympathetic ear.

Too many in education have yelled for higher teacher pay without explaining why, without looking closely at the issue (in my home state of SC, the average teacher salary is far above the average salary in the state, though I believe that is still well below the appropriate pay for a professional), without admitting that pay within a socialistic system *cannot* be comparable with salaries in the free market. Too many have yelled for lowering the student-teacher ratio in classrooms as if the lowering itself will address anything; the truth is lowering student-teacher ratio without changing instructional and assessment practices will accomplish nothing. Too many have yelled for more funding to purchase computers, though we have done the same thing with other technological innovations over and over—radios, TVs, VCRs, laser disks, and the good ol' green-screen Apples—with little evidence of progress other than of the electronic kind.

If the print and radio media are getting it wrong, if even educators massage the numbers for their own gain, then what does an educational honesty about numbers look like? How can we know when the numbers don't lie? Let's look at a discussion of two of the favorite numbers-laden areas of education debated in America almost daily—school funding and student poverty, both of which provide educators with a vast array of statistical data and educational research.

"Foolishness, Dangerous Nonsense, and Real Correlates of State Differences in Achievement"—even Bruce J. Biddle (1997) titles his discussion with many clues to how we must address educational debates filled with numbers: Avoiding foolishness (oversimplification) and addressing the real (complexities that defy dead-end conclusions). Biddle begins his discussion of school funding among the states and student poverty by directly admitting that much of the discussion around those topics is muddled by political agendas and misguided assumptions, namely that educators are incompetent or lazy (much as Williams, 2003, implied).

Honesty in the educational debate requires that we first bring to light the assumptions, the biases, and the status of *what we know*. Biddle (1997) asserts that concerning school funding and student poverty, the research is lacking in many ways—data on funding allowing arguments on conflicting sides to champion their causes with plenty of numbers, data on poverty so convoluted that solid conclusions about the impact of poverty are nearly impossible. He explains that the research itself must pass serious scrutiny before we can even begin to draw conclusions from the data and hope to implement any changes that may benefit children. Not only is education complex, but also is conducting research and drawing legitimate conclusions from the findings. The truth about any educational research is that identifying *single* factors to draw any cause-and-effect relationships is nearly impossible and is always messy and tentative.

Finally, Biddle (1997) attempts to make the fairest pronouncements that he can about school funding and poverty in relationship to education. He shows that if we look closely at data surrounding NAEP math data from 1996, we can begin to raise questions (not draw clear, demonstrative conclusions) and cast doubt on the political solutions to educational problems that appear to be linked to funding and poverty. Biddle's conclusions aren't very earth-shattering or sexy; we didn't see them on the front pages of newspapers. "This study shows that we have more questions and some things to experiment with" just doesn't sing like "SC is 50th in the nation in SATs, again." And Biddle's tentative scientific stance, the proper and honest stance of a researcher, doesn't carry the fire and brimstone certainty of a talk-radio host deeming all schools a liberal blight on society.

Politicians, pundits, and the media long for sound bites supported by the gravity of numbers. But human endeavors such as teaching simply do not lend themselves to such, if we are being honest. Numbers pulled from testing and demographics can be our friends if we understand that those numbers are mere descriptions and reductions of this messy thing we call living.

• • •

As a scientist and a journalist, Chet Raymo (1998) pulls full circle the problems and ironies faced by educators in a sea of politics, the media, and simplistic perceptions of numbers, research, and ultimately science:

> And this, it seems to me, is what is behind much of the wide popular distrust of science: ignorance. As a people, we live in a civilization that is based upon science, but we know very little about science. . . . Science requires enlightened community criticism, community guardianship, and community engagement, and these must be led by scholars and intellectuals. (pp. 170–171)

His points about the American psyche and science parallel the concerns I have raised here with the public discussion of education. I would simply echo his call for educators to lead the education debate, to raise our voices above the numbers.

 # PART 2

Numbers Games in the Classroom
and against the Classroom

> One of the basic elements of the relationship between oppressor and oppressed is *prescription*. Every prescription represents the imposition of one individual's choice upon another, transforming the consciousness of the person prescribed to into one that conforms with the prescriber's consciousness.
>
> —Paulo Freire, *Pedagogy of the Oppressed*

 THREE

The Numbers and Forces behind Teaching Practices

Regardless of the foolishness educators suffer from politicians, pundits, journalists, and misguided parents (and all those who pay taxes to run our schools) the truth is that we need to look long and hard at the actual teaching and learning happening in our classrooms. Many forces *attempt* to dictate the teaching of America's children, but no mandates can insure that anything actually occurs there that is required.

One fact of schooling is that teachers often do as they please when they shut their doors. The greatest influences on the reality of the classroom tend to be what each teacher believes and assumes about teaching and assessing, what each teacher believes is required of that teacher, and what each teacher feels a moral and professional (both *to* the profession and for the preservation of a job) obligation to do. Far too often, teacher practices are gut-driven, even in the face of clear evidence to the contrary—much as millions and millions gathered to celebrate the turning of the millennium on the night of December 31, 1999, one year too soon.

The voices of teachers in the field are ample evidence of the folly of mandating teacher behavior. Esme Raji Codell (1999) realizes such during her first year of teaching:

> The closed-door teacher anarchy I suggested seems so scary in theory, but in reality, I see it already exists. In my opinion, the prefabricated curriculum and board mandates that are concocted to hide this state of affairs can work in two ways. They can be benign suggestions that make talented inventors

out of teachers. Or they can make it so people who don't have anything to share can still work, since their scripts are made up for them. Nobody really knows which is happening when the teacher closes the door. . . . Only, I wonder if [those dictating teaching] can see that the efforts to try to regulate teaching could limit learning as much as insure it. . . . You can't test what sort of teacher someone will be, because testing what someone knows isn't the same as what someone is able to share. (pp. 139–140)

Yes, pressures on teachers to implement and perform are great, possibly more intense today than ever. But as I have discussed in Chapter One, often what is true and provable is quite powerless in the face of assumptions, beliefs, and the momentum of tradition and habit. That is equally true for teachers as it is for the average American. Public school classrooms are impacted daily by the influence of our standardized tests and by numbers assumptions—the measurement and assessment habits of teachers.

Covering Content and Planning for the Future

With the momentum begun by *A Nation at Risk*, U.S. public classroom teachers have felt an increasing pressure to cover content—the inevitable result of all the many Back-to-Basics movements that have plagued progressive educators throughout the last century, a tired approach that now claims to leave no child behind. Olson (2003a) explains that schools have continuously claimed to raise the bar throughout the last 2 decades by increasing the content that courses cover, thus seemingly increasing the rigor of the curriculum. Compared to a couple decades ago, more students are in courses labeled "honors" or "advanced," and those same courses are advertised as more highly content-rich. Increasing content is easy to show with scope-and-sequence curriculum guides and easy to measure through standardized and so-called objective testing; as well, content coverage is simple to organize in traditional lesson plans and easy to document for accountability. Sadly, increasing content and ratcheting up the coverage of that content serves no one well—not teachers, not students, not the American public.

Along with this drive to cover knowledge, teachers have been for decades pressured to prepare students for the future, more often than not, for work. Eisner (2003/2004) admits that such an objective appears reasonable. Yet, this purpose of schooling, one Dewey (1938) challenged, proves to be ineffective and limiting, though it fits nicely with political and market goals:

> School curriculums based on the preparatory conception of education are often intellectually irrelevant or become little more than hoops through which students learn to jump in order to move ahead. . . . The last thing we need is a one-size-fits-all curriculum with one single set of goals for everyone. (Eisner, 2003/2004, p. 8)

The future, it seems, is unknowable; what is best and right for each child is equally unknowable. No matter how often politicians or business leaders cry for preparatory education, it is futile. Yet, more teachers than not would claim that is their purpose in the classroom.

These driving forces—content coverage and schooling for preparing students for the future—are reinforced by and contribute to the many numbers games played somewhat mindlessly by teachers. Those numbers games, by the way, are as often the result of teacher choice as the result of mandates from above.

Reseeing the Classroom—
Quantifying (and Confusing) Means and Ends

When I stand before my graduate education classes, teachers or students soon to become teachers, I have begun asking whom we consider smart. How would Gandhi have performed on the SAT? And further, in America, who is considered successful? Does any person's net worth void any relevance about her intelligence? Do numbers from testing? Does any set body of facts truly show intelligence?

Erroneously, many believe that during the 1900s, American education in general, and classrooms in particular, were dominated by the Progressive Era. Yet in reality the century was marked by traditional approaches to teaching, learning, and assessing (most often with a solid focus on content coverage and objective measurements of learning). From 1906 until 1971, Lou LaBrant worked as a teacher of reading and writing, espousing and practicing student-centered and experimental approaches to teaching and learning. Two aspects of her life and work seem relevant as we consider what teachers should do in their classrooms while under the burden of high-stakes testing and misguided legislation: first, a series of Back-to-Basics movements (that included standards and standardized testing) and second, her stance *as an English teacher* to eliminate English as a content course of study. For 65 years as a teacher, LaBrant directly fought against numbers games and for students.

During her life, which ended in 1991, LaBrant worked through and witnessed at least three or four movements similar to NCLB now, complete with raised standards and high-stakes testing. At the end of her life she watched from a distance the politically corrupt *A Nation at Risk* report. As an educator concerned with authentic student learning, learning for understanding, she documented through her published writings the inherent flaws in content-bound standards and standardized testing. In short, all standards movements have limited student learning—reducing teaching, learning, and assessing to the most superficial aspects, such as numbers easily displayed in charts and graphs.

Further LaBrant embodied a stance that insures authentic learning by students, a stance never fully embraced by education as an institution, a stance rare in the classrooms across America. LaBrant's first major appointment was on the initial faculty of the University School of Ohio State University where she proposed that English not be offered as a course; all teachers should be teaching reading and writing in the context of their content, she argued. Essentially, LaBrant and many progressives, from John Dewey to Howard Gardner, have asserted that *what* we teach matters very little; content is relatively inconsequential. The content of the curriculum is a means, not an end, to student understanding. English, to LaBrant, for example, is the teaching of reading and writing, the fostering of valuable performances of understanding, but not a set of knowledge to be imposed on passive learners—as content is more often than not treated in American schools, especially when accountability is high.

• • •

That education and its periodic swings toward standards and accountability have never sincerely addressed deep learning, learning for understanding (instead choosing the manageable, the superficial, and the quantifiable) seems to be a tremendous and damning claim. But except for the isolated classroom, the isolated school, the institution that is American public education does deserve that criticism. How has that happened? And what about those glory days, those good old days of educational success? Though not simple, three explanations show how we have piddled with the manageable and the superficial while always ignoring authentic learning—political control of education, greed (by testing companies and ambitious educators), and the unschooled mind. As for the good old days, that is easy to explain; they never existed for education.

As noted in the last chapter, Bracey (1997a, 1997b) has documented that both politicians and educators disparage education for their benefit, often waving stacks of data to support their claims. Recently, the same process is occurring with school-choice initiatives; educational debate becomes a political investment that must be manageable, thus superficial; and numbers work well within that dynamic. It is politically, though not educationally, expedient to list a content-oriented, scope-and-sequence curriculum, to force teachers to teach only that factual material, and then to administer a selected-response test (bubbles and a number-two pencil) on facts.

Further, Coles (2000) discusses the perennial debate over reading instruction; this issue reveals a second explanation for our educational failures, greed. As we have seen, instructional materials, instructional programs, and testing are money-making ventures for the savvy entrepreneur. While I am not claiming that these are conspiracies, I am arguing that these phenomena do exist. As well, I believe Howard Gardner (1991) has been dealing with the broader issue that allows these misguided influences on education to thrive unchecked, the unschooled mind; he also refers to the 5-year-old mind-set in subsequent works over the past decade in a number of contexts including leadership. Leaders often speak simplistically to the public at large because it works. While Gardner has offered data on graduates from highly prestigious universities and their simplistic (and inaccurate) scientific understandings after receiving their degrees in science, several anecdotal examples exist every day that suggest how often society *as a whole* functions at the 5-year-old level, a simplified level of misconception such as I explored in Chapter One.

Politics, greed, and the unschooled mind have all contributed to an educational system that is manageable and superficial. Further, we have become so mired in that system that we have yet to pause and ask two crucial questions: Is standardization compatible with American democracy? And what is *knowing*? These are crucial questions for the individual teacher to address as she faces a class of students or as he contemplates what to teach and how to assess that learning.

With no hesitation, I can quickly state that standardization is completely un-American. Our standards and testing movements are the antitheses of educating young people to be free, to be empowered, and to be full participants in a democracy. Only instruction and curriculum designed for student understanding and authentic assessment *practiced* in the classroom can lead to the free and the empowered. But what is learning for understanding: What roles exist for content coverage and testing in our classrooms? And how might a teacher face this question in a numbers-laden society?

• • •

Our greatest failure in a quest for student understanding has been our dependence on suspect measures of student learning. The content-orientation and the objective format of assessment have combined with the single-sitting implementation of testing to produce superficial evidence concerning student understanding. Gardner (1991, 1999a) has explained that traditional student learning is often easily supplanted by simplistic "gut" knowledge and that society's obsession with trivia as knowledge (consider television shows like "Jeopardy" or "Who Wants to Be a Millionaire?") reflects our acceptance of superficial evidence as proof of understanding. Are teachers' own perceptions much different from the average person's conceptions, of learning, of understanding?

This superficial approach has sprung from three curricular errors—packing the curriculum with too many facts to be covered in too little time, teaching and assessing for rote memorization, and valuing the coverage of curriculum over the learning by the student. Dempster (1993) has promoted reducing the American curriculum, noting the relatively smaller curriculums (and textbooks) of other countries. Kralovec and Buell (2001) add that schooling such as in Japan has greater student achievement with less, especially in terms of homework and material covered. Even our own numbers' mania disputes our default solution to raising standards—cover more content!

With our overcrowded curriculum, one that grows each year, even in schools that have reduced contact time per course (as with block scheduling that often lowers a course from 180 hours to 120 hours), we insure that teachers require and students achieve only rote memorization. Gardner (1991, 1999a) feels that more time should be spent focusing deeply on selected and rich areas of content with an emphasis placed on process (learning to be a learner, learning to be an expert, learning to see the complexity in knowing) and engagement by students. In his book, *The Disciplined Mind*, Gardner (1999a) offers several examples—suggesting that dealing with a major historical event, such as the Holocaust, over a large unit, delving deeply, is far more important than covering the entire timeline of historical events in a course. Yet, teaching and learning for understanding require assessment philosophies and practices that are far less manageable, far less easily reduced to numbers.

"Indeed, the pursuit of basic skills may sometimes be counterproductive," explains Gardner (1991), adding, "In the effort to make sure that students 'cover' the curriculum and are prepared for various milestones and tests, teachers may inadvertently be undermining more crucial educational goals" (p. 187). Sadly, many teachers in many classrooms, under the duress of meeting standards, map out their entire year's instruction (before ever seeing a child) based on state or district curriculum and follow that daily schedule despite how much their students learn, how much their students understand, or how much their students are engaged. A single example, although not unique to its field, is the teaching of math. Math courses are often portrayed as highly dependent on sequence, lesson one building for lesson two, and so forth. Yet every year of my teaching, students complain about a never-ending process in their math courses that bowls straight over them: Homework on a new lesson *before* the new material is discussed in class, class work for a day or three (usually involving work at the board), then a test on the chapter, followed by the next chapter the next class meeting *regardless of what students make on the previous assessment*. The goal of many classrooms is to cover material and to document that coverage, not to insure student understanding of big ideas—all driven by each teacher's perception of what should be taught, how it should be covered, and how it should be assessed. Numbers must be gathered and reports filed.

• • •

As we eventually answer, What should we teach?, we must begin with seeing the big picture:

[T]he focus is on process rather than on product. The student is asked to bring about change in herself rather than to wait for change to be imposed from the outside (or to believe that change cannot occur at all) and to accept that assessment may be the burden not of the teacher primarily but of the learner herself. (Gardner, 1991, p. 243)

On my educational landscape, questions are more important than answers; knowledge and, more important, understanding should evolve from the constant probing of such questions. . . . I organize my presentation around [what is true, beautiful, and good] because they motivate individuals to learn about and understand their world, and because, frankly, I reject a world in which individuals cease to pursue these essential questions just because they do not permit unequivocal resolution. (Gardner, 1999a, p. 24)

The direct answer to "What should we teach?" is, "It just matters very little; content is a means, not an end." We must reframe the question to *how* we teach whatever we choose to teach, and *why* we teach whatever we choose to teach, and ultimately *how* we measure and quantify (if at all) that understanding. Teaching for student understanding is not content specific; it is what students are able to do with any set of facts, any text, or any human or natural creation that matters.

When we eliminate a concern for content-for-content's-sake, we actually create a more rigorous curriculum (Gardner, 1999a, p. 44) because we are focusing all lessons around essential questions that can be wrestled with through hundreds of idiosyncratic sets of content. When what we teach is reformed around essential questions, big concepts, teachers must come to embrace the open-ended nature of planning, of learning, and of assessing. *We cannot know what we need to do the next day as a teacher, and not all students will learn the same and at the same rate.* Daily behavioral objects and pacing guides along with standardized testing are of no educational value (though they serve political agendas well) when learning for understanding is our goal. The basics are acquired during the journey of learning as students discover the need to master those basics. If students learn only to garner a score, a grade, a number, then learning has not occurred; the coerced child does not grow up to be an empowered adult who fulfills the obligations of a citizen in a democracy.

If classroom teachers are to be freed from the shackles of the numbers games they play in their own classrooms, they must resee the big concerns of public education. Briefly, that reseeing must include:

1. *Nature of learning.* As we strive for learning for understanding and for authentic assessment, we have to make a shift from behaviorism to constructivism as our paradigm for learning (Kralovec & Buell, 2001; Brooks & Brooks, 1999; Lambert, et al., 1995). This shift includes a valuing of student engagement and an appreciation for student mistakes.

2. *Curriculum.* The scope-and-sequence curriculum that lists content to be covered must become defunct; we must begin to

create curriculum guides that offer as a resource a myriad of content questions and problems that teachers can implement as needed depending on the makeup of each class encountered, each student engaged.

3. *Instructional behavioral objectives.* These too should become defunct since they are educationally unsound. Preplanned and scripted lessons are not teaching and do not produce student understanding. Daily, targeted activities that can be adjusted midstream and targeted units of study will serve students and teachers best and allow for a focus on the students and their evolving understanding; again, content coverage cannot be allowed to dictate classroom dynamics.

4. *Assessment and standardization.* Like curriculum content, assessment is a means to learning, not a system of labeling by quantifying as it now stands. And standardization of learning by students must be uniformly rejected as un-American and as countereducational.

The concern for higher standards and accountability can be resolved by making rigor our basic educational goal, not a set of facts that must be covered and quantified. Knowing the years of the Holocaust are of little value to anyone until that person begins to understand the horror and magnitude of human cruelty and suffering—and until that person begins to develop a sense of human empathy for all people suffering at the hands of the cruel in the past *and* during each day that we live. And no set of numbers can truly capture or express that horror; the number murdered during the Holocaust pales in comparison to Kurt Vonnegut's *Slaughterhouse-Five* or the words of Anne Frank as she lived and perished during the Holocaust.

• • •

Botstein (1997) has challenged American education to resee the American high school. The traditional approach is less rigorous; it "underestimat[es] what children can learn," Botstein argues, because of the emphasis on content and measurement (p. 44). His call includes issues raised here—the importance of questions, the need for student skepticism, the value of mistakes in learning, the failure of restrictive educational standards, and the need to teach students first and foremost to be intrinsically motivated learners. These are calls you will

Numbers Games

never hear uttered by a politician or a textbook company or a testing company. These calls are incredibly difficult to implement and measure, but they are the only changes worth pursuing.

Knowing and understanding our existence as humans is an evolving thing; we are constantly adjusting our knowing. Traditional approaches to what we should teach portray the world as a static thing sprung into a crystalline state from some ancient place with little or no human involvement. Students are best served, as is society, when they learn that we are tentative knowers at best, espousing our warranted assertions one day, realizing we may be saying something quite or subtly different the next day, or even before the sun goes down. Classroom teachers must face their assumptions about the role of content (traditionally as an end, as *the* goal of instruction, though more effectively as a means) and about the purposes and formats of assessment.

The Weight of Numbers in the Classroom

Standardized tests do without doubt greatly impact teacher practices ("High School Exit Assessments," 2003; Egan, 2003). Further, evidence certainly supports that those teacher practices profoundly affect student learning and performance ("The Effect of Classroom Practice on Student Achievement," 2003). Since standards and standardized tests impact and reinforce teacher assumptions and fears, a dangerous cycle for student learning exists in classrooms. A growing body of research shows that our test mania is negatively impacting student learning because of its impact on classroom practices (Langland, 2003; Amrein & Berliner, 2002; Neill, 2003).

As the door closes more tightly on learning in our classrooms, some students and parents are beginning to revolt; some families and students are simply refusing to take the high-stakes tests (Galehouse, 2003; Torres, 2003; Harrison, 2003). Assumptions, misconceptions, and traditions are difficult to face and nearly impossible to overcome. But when we look directly into classrooms—not at the numbers drawn from those students, but *eye to eye* with those children—we must reconsider some of those issues such as the role of capitalism, consumerism, and humans as products in the teaching of children.

Ohanian (2003) directly confronts the capitalistic influences and assumptions that impact the classrooms in U.S. schools. Similar to my own argument, she accuses many of approaching educational problems with a Cycloptic tunnel vision that allows only market ideology to address any concern; competition, apparently, could remove warts or even raise the dead. The SAT is overly simplistic in its dichotomous perception of the world, and standardized testing doesn't produce thinkers, she explains. Coupled with ideological blind spots, educational mandates often carry political agendas that somewhat carelessly reduce teaching to mere content coverage in order to appease tests. And speaking of the tests, Ohanian also recognizes that the cult of the bell-shaped curve, the *imposed* bell-shaped curve, forces some students to fail; no room is left for no child to be left behind by standardized tests that are slaves to a certain kind of statistical truth. And as we shall see, some classroom teachers apply that same false bell-shaped curve mentality to the classroom, insuring failure there as well.

The students are the ones who suffer under the weight of these misconceptions and assumptions. Cheney, McMillan, and Schwartzman (1997) along with Lewis (2003) add to this concern that we treat students with a dualistic and contradictory view that is grounded in capitalism as well. Students are being spoken of as products *and* as consumers (often along with their parents). The perception of the student as product is dehumanizing both for the student and for teachers who are forced to see their students as fruits of their labor, not as young human beings who are unique and *alive*. The student-as-consumer mentality is directly contrary to a system that respects professional expertise in the teacher; in the consumer-dictates-all market metaphor, the consumer is the expert: "Who's paying your salary? So do as I say!" In many fields, that metaphor is simply asinine. If we carelessly apply the market metaphor, the student-as-consumer analogy to fields such as teaching, we relinquish educational expertise to the student (or the parents). So do we really believe that students and parents should dictate classroom practices; that's going to raise educational standards?

Again, the truth is that sometimes the market paradigm, the competition model that involves consumers and measurable product quality simply does not apply; and if we force such models where they don't belong, we actually cause more harm than good. Such is the case in our public school classrooms where capitalist ideologues and greedy entrepreneurs are set to prey on beleaguered teachers and essentially powerless and voiceless students (Molnar, 2003/2004).

Should Teachers Bow to Tests? No

A revamped SAT lurks on the horizon along with a growing concern for NAEP data on student achievement in math, reading, and now writing. The assault is number rich, and classroom practices will certainly change under the pressure, unless we shout loud enough and educators claim the classrooms for student understanding.

"Inside the New SATs" teases the cover of *Time* magazine (October 27, 2003). Covering part of the face of a young man holding the required No. 2 pencil is a mock multiple-choice question that reads, "The big test is being retooled. The changes could: (A) Favor girls over boys, (B) Affect how we teach English in high schools, (C) Make SAT scores more subjective, (D) Create an uproar among teachers and parents, (E) All of the above." The provocative answer is of course (E).

This discussion of changes in the SAT comes on the heels of the National Assessment of Educational Progress (NAEP) data from 2002 concerning student writing achievement and The College Board's report through its National Commission on Writing in America's Schools and Colleges. The NAEP writing data have led to some fairly public hand wringing about the writing abilities of students and the quality of writing instruction in our English/language arts classrooms, and the new SAT will impact writing instruction by including both a brief composition section along with a selected-response grammar and usage section.

The changes in the SAT and the NAEP writing results should give educators and the public pause concerning how curriculum, instruction, and assessment in our classrooms are shaped and by what. Currently, public schools are frantically treading water in the rising tide of federal and state mandates driven by standards and high-stakes testing; teachers and students alike are drowning in numbers. Most of that legislation insures that a large percentage of schools *appear* to be failures and a large number of teachers *appear* to be under-qualified—not to improve public education, but to discredit it in the public eye. Less obvious and equally as disturbing is that both the impending changes to the SAT and the proclamations made about the 2002 NAEP writing test results reveal another significant river feeding the flood drowning our schools, our students, and our teachers: *Curriculum, instruction, and assessment in our schools are being dictated indirectly but significantly by the decisions made in the designing and implementing of standardized commercial tests; in effect, the number gatherers are running the classrooms.* Yes, NAEP writing data from 2002 and the next manifestation of the SAT in 2005, for example, do matter in our quest to reform classroom instruction, but not in ways that are being discussed by politicians, educrats, and the media.

• • •

While writing performance and assessment are at the far end of traditional academic areas ill suited for standardized testing, all high-stakes standardized testing is greatly limited in what it can offer teachers and students along with its consistently detrimental impact on teaching and learning in the classroom (Abrams & Madaus, 2003). Standardized commercial testing provides narrow data on student ability or learning (and heavily distorted data on school and state-wide educational quality) and carries inappropriate influence over the curriculum and instruction in our schools, especially in terms of assessment; teacher practices are inordinately mandated by testing, at the expense of best practice supported by decades of research.

In the big picture, those who mandate the running of schools and much of the general public just have things all wrong about what knowing means and how to measure that knowing. In Barbara King-solver's *Animal Dreams* (1990), Codi returns to her hometown; she is a medical school dropout and a drifting spirit. Contrary to her own plans, she falls in love with Loyd, her brief and careless lover from high school who leaves her pregnant (though he never knows of the pregnancy, a child Codi loses before birth). As an adult, Loyd is a train engineer, and in Chapter 23, he is telling Codi about a recent and difficult maneuver he has conducted with a particularly long and heavy train. "'Nobody can just tell you how to do that hill?'" Codi asks Loyd, who replies, "'No, because every train's different on every hill. Every single run is a brand-new job. You have to learn the feel of it'" (p. 295).

Kingsolver (1990), in this scene, offers a nice metaphor for the chasm that exists in education between the learning and assessing of the purely academic (often we cover material that we know will be tested, and how it will be tested, primarily as an exercise in account-ability) and the learning and assessing of the real, of the holistic and chaotic things of living; we deal in the measurable although the im-portant things in life are beyond quantifying. For Loyd, his tests are the actual piloting of the train, each journey both an experience and a test, each journey unique; in life we rarely can separate the learning from the tests, though in school we often require students to learn merely to prepare for a test. The stuff of school manifests itself in the real world in whole and chaotic ways; every second before us, our living, is unpredictable, as unique as each train run for Loyd. Yet, those who legislate the running of schools are obsessed with prescribing what is to be learned, dictating how curriculum is to be taught, forcing all behavior into one-size-fits-all templates, and quantifying all learning through the most narrow and fragmented, though statistically manageable, means of assessment available.

Writing—like art, band, chorus, or athletics—serves as a vivid example of the inherent inadequacy of standardized, multiple-choice high-stakes testing (though possibly no worse than standardized testing in other forms, which will be explored later) to measure whole activities. Popham (2001a), joined by a number of others (Coles, 2000; Kohn, 2000; Abrams & Madaus, 2003), explains that the essential nature of standardized testing, possibly best typified by the traditional SAT, has many inherent weaknesses in terms of gathering data, in terms of reflecting both an individual student's knowledge and any group of students' achievements, and in terms of how the data are interpreted and how those interpretations are used. Popham argues that standardized testing fails when it becomes the curriculum, teaching to the test, and that standardized testing fails when it becomes high stakes, test scores being the sole source for awarding student's credit or promotions and test scores being used to judge the quality of schools or state-wide school systems.

Just as The College Board has explained, Popham (2001a) and most experts in the business of large-scale testing warn that making comparisons and judgments about the quality of schools and school systems based on a single set of testing data is tenuous at best and greatly misleading at worst. Yet, politicians and the media fuel year after year the general public's need to rank the quality of each state's school system simply by comparing statewide average SAT scores. We rank and judge, but never fully ask what real relationship exists among best practice in classroom instruction and assessment, the abilities needed to function and excel in life, and the narrow format and purposes of the SAT. Teachers' faces are usually the only faces on those proclaimed failures.

Those who are expert and experienced in the field of large-scale standardized testing have begun to provide ample evidence that standardized tests and testing data are inappropriate for the current accountability mania today in the politicized arena of public education, as the sole indicator of student or school quality. Additionally, we have growing evidence that standardized testing has its most profoundly negative effect on holistic endeavors such as reading and writing—particularly when the test becomes the *de facto* curriculum in our schools, the guide for classroom instructional practices, and the template for all our classroom assessment.

Hillocks (2003), Coles (2000), Freedman (1995), and Mabry (1999) offer a solid core of evidence that high-stakes standardized testing is incredibly harmful to reading and writing instruction and student achievement. When standardized tests are traditional multiple-choice exams, then reading and writing get reduced to fragmented and inauthentic worksheet activities: Students reading merely to choose A, B, C, D, or E; students not actually composing at all on a "writing" exam, but scanning other people's sentences for errors in grammar, mechanics, and usage (where test makers are prone to deal with only the most arcane aspects of those surface features). Reading and writing instruction and classroom assessment begin to mirror high-stakes tests, thus reducing and even eliminating students actually reading and composing in our classrooms in any holistic or authentic ways.

More disturbing still is that even when our state-designed or commercial assessments have moved to what appear to be more open-ended forms of testing in which students do compose original essays (as many state assessments do, as the new SAT will include), Freedman (1995), Mabry (1999), and Hillocks (2003) have uncovered that writing required on standardized testing shares the exact same negative impacts on instruction, assessment, and learning that the more often maligned selected-response testing produces. Even when students actually compose on tests, the rubrics and sample essays provided by the test designers for information become the curriculum; they become templates for students to fulfill. If webbing appears on the state exam *as one form of brainstorming*, then it becomes *the only* form of brainstorming allowed the next year in classroom after classroom.

• • •

Now, dangers lurk ahead for teachers because of the decisions being made in the changes to the SAT in writing and because of the reactions to the NAEP 2002 writing exam results. Though not laughable, it is somewhat ironic that by The College Board's own admission, the SAT has never been any better an indicator of college success than simple high school GPAs—"Overall, high school grades predict freshman GPA[s] slightly better than do SAT scores" (Camara & Echternacht, 2000, p. 4). The difference is GPAs are free and the SAT costs both students and schools large amounts of needed funds and time. The time investment for the SAT grows yearly from the inordinate amount of SAT-prep work being implemented as part of the curriculum in content classrooms.

Of course, the sole purpose of the SAT is to predict college success; it never has been intended by The College Board as an indicator of the quality of a school or a state's school system, and to The College Board's credit, it has made numerous, though mild, attempts to dissuade the annual ranking of a state's school system by average SAT scores. To maintain its false aura of predictability, though, and its annual income, The College Board recentered SAT scoring in the not-so-distant past and now is greatly overhauling its flagship exam. Additionally, this impending retooling has come during the rising tide of high-stakes standardized testing in the U.S., with troubling data that show state-mandated high-stakes tests as quite weak in predicting college success, especially in areas such as writing (Cavanaugh, 2003; Conley, 2003). We cannot ignore as well that The College Board's own National Commission on Writing in America's Schools and Colleges has conveniently reacted to the NAEP writing results from 2002 simultaneously with the new SAT, adding actual student composing on the test. Americans are quick to embrace the idea that testing will solve any educational weakness; again, we are eager to weigh the pig *as if regular weighing will make the pig fatter.*

• • •

A decade ago in the pages of *English Journal*, Warner (1993) lamented the persistent practice by English teachers to address writing instruction in the most inauthentic and ineffective ways (notably the traditional obsession with isolated grammar instruction in the form of grammar text exercises and worksheet-like tests) as if grammar knowledge were the goal of ELA and not fostering students as writers (much as analogy instruction has been a central part of isolated vocabulary instruction as if analogies were a goal unto themselves). Although decades of evidence have confirmed that such isolated grammar-mania does not improve student writing and does erode student motivation to write and the surface feature and content quality of student writing (Hillocks, 1995; Weaver, 1996), Warner conceded then that "[m]any [teachers] believe the teaching of grammar is necessary if students are to 'do well' on those standardized tests" (p.

79). "We have to do analogies because of the SAT," we might also hear echoing down the halls of our schools.

High-stakes testing was not as fever-pitched a decade ago as today, but Warner (1993) notes that classroom instruction was more often than not impacted negatively for the purposes of addressing a test, while best practice in instruction was simply ignored. When standardized tests determine student credit for a course or promotion, student graduation, or student scholarships, the tests themselves become the ends of schooling and at least overshadow, if not eradicate, our real aims as educators—students' growth as scholars and citizens in a free society (Abrams & Madaus, 2003).

When challenged to implement best practice, educators use as a political scapegoat time and again their obligation to address standardized tests no matter how weak or ill designed those tests may be. While for decades vocabulary texts and English teachers have touted the power and value in deciphering analogies (a significant part of the SAT before the 2005 changes), it will not take long for such practices to disappear. By 2005, the SAT will no longer require what amounts to nothing more than a clever intellectual game, a game that manifests itself not at all in our daily lives in any form similar to the testing of analogies. Again, the test becomes the goal; it dictates what matters, at the expense of *what matters*.

Also in the new version, the SAT will include a writing section requiring students actually to compose brief essays; that change upon first blush seems wonderful to those who teach students to write and advocate authentic assessment. But a closer inspection shows that the SAT will also include an isolated grammar and usage selected-response section, thus creating a perceived need for isolated grammar instruction (most administrators and teachers will assume that the only and best way to prepare for such a test is isolated grammar instruction, especially if that instruction and assessment can be formatted the same as the new SAT testing format) and creating an implication that isolated grammar instruction is writing instruction, both of which have been refuted for decades by the best advocates for writing instruction (Weaver, 1996; Williams, 1990). Little progress has been made so far in curbing the wealth of direct grammar instruction in English classes, so this change in the verbal SAT heralds a serious setback in classroom practices, ironically all in the name of raising standards.

Further, the addition of a composing section on the SAT will, as

Hillocks (2003) and Mabry (1999) have shown, actually further damage what little effective composing instruction takes place in schools today. Sample SAT essays and the rubrics used for scoring those essays will ultimately become the imposed curriculum for writing instruction in our schools, and students will be dealt another deadly blow in the name of testing, accountability, and the political and financial aspirations of a few. The samples provided by The College Board will quickly translate into templates for teachers to require and for students to follow; we will continue to have little concern for students becoming writers, but we will call for students to write as the SAT mandates.

Ultimately, classroom teachers should pry themselves loose from the grips of the SAT altogether. What little value it offers, as revealed in The College Board's own research, does not justify the time and cost incurred by students and teachers alike. But until then we must acknowledge that the changes made to the proposed 2005 SAT are destined to be highly and negatively influential on the instruction and assessment our children will encounter in classrooms across the U.S. That impact will certainly do far more harm than good unless teachers confront standardized tests as false goals of our teaching young people to be empowered.

• • •

While the SAT has garnered what I would characterize as an unfounded authoritative status for quantifying student achievement, determining college entrance and college scholarships, and labeling the quality of our schools, the NAEP quite boldly proclaims itself to be "The Nation's Report Card" (See the National Center for Educational Statistics Web site, http://nces.ed.gov/, for information and data from the NAEP 2002 writing exam). The NAEP writing test, similar to the addition of actual composing on the 2005 SAT, would appear to be a move in the right direction to teachers since it requires students to compose on the exam and since the 2002 data have spurred a call for more and better writing instruction, notably The College Board's own report from the National Commission on Writing in America's Schools and Colleges. Should we be suspicious when the same company that changes its product also issues a report showing a need for such a change?

The National Commission on Writing in America's Schools and Colleges has also jumped in with its "The Neglected 'R': The Need for a Writing Revolution." Further still, the National Writing Project

(NWP) has contributed its considerable (and well-deserved) status to the many reactions about these standardized measurements of student writing and the need for improving writing instruction. Regardless of all the political and financial implications of this situation (though it shares many qualities with the Open Court reading program and the implied federal endorsement of its research-based materials), the NAEP writing test from 2002 has spurred a much-needed discussion of writing ability and writing instruction in America.

Yet, the NAEP 2002 data on student writing have also been at the center of this most recent target-of-the-week in the bashing of U.S. public schools: "Oh, no! Our students can't write!" we are yelling (once again; take a look at any point in the past when we said anything different about our children's writing abilities—or any ability, for that matter). But few people, if any, have raised two important issues about the data and the debate concerning student writing ability spurred by the NAEP results and reflected in the comments by national organizations, politicians, and the media along with changes in major tests:

- Are the writing prompts and rubrics used in the NAEP assessment credible in light of best practice in writing instruction and assessment? In other words, is the test itself beyond criticism as a solid tool for measuring student writing ability?

- Should we be attempting to assess and quantify student writing, or any of the learning achieved by students, in the standardized, one-shot ways in which the NAEP tests and reports have manifested themselves?

I have to ask, "Do 2002 NAEP writing results deserve such power over the reforming of instruction and assessment in our schools?" And my answer is the same as my response to "Should we be teaching to the new writing portion of the SAT?" We must say, "No."

The NAEP writing test shows clearly that when we force writing into a standardized testing format, little that is good comes from that essential mistake; despite the best efforts of NAEP, the SAT, or even The College Board's own excellent Advanced Placement testing, most things worth knowing simply cannot be tested in standardized ways with any real value—especially when the standardized, one-shot test becomes the sole indicator of student achievement and the *de facto* curriculum. As noted above, a great deal of research shows that writing prompts, scoring rubrics, and sample essays all combine to recreate indirectly the writing curriculum of our schools; further, writing instruction and assessment also are controlled by both the format and the content of the tests as well as by the rubrics used to score those tests.

Hillocks (2003) and Mabry (1999) show that when assessment rubrics and sample essays become templates for students to fill, we have lost any chance at authentic or valuable writing instruction; the power in the test means that teachers abdicate their expertise as writing instructors, and it means that administrators reduce further their expectations of teachers being the experts in their classrooms. Both teachers and students become slaves to complying with artificial requirements for an act that is highly idiosyncratic and unpredictable. Learning is an act of discovery, not a formula to be imprinted onto each child.

The 2002 NAEP writing test, ironically, fails as an authority on writing instruction and assessment to those who want to teach students to write in meaningful ways, but it offers education and educators some important red flags that could lead us out of the black hole of measurement and standardized testing. First, when we look at the NAEP writing highlights provided by NCES, it should make us wonder if there is a danger in data overload; the data from standardized testing tend to come in the form of numbers, but is often thin in any detailed data that may be useful for individual teachers to address individual student needs. Can all those numbers and all those disaggregations possibly do teachers any good in their daily pursuit of teaching each child they encounter? Can holistic acts be reduced to numbers in effective and meaningful ways? Can it possibly do any one teacher of any one child any good to know that grade four Asian/Pacific Islander students scored on average a 167 on the 2002 NAEP writing test? I think not.

Teachers must shout that reducing either an individual student's writing performance or any group of students' writing performances to numbers offers no help for instruction and can only offer great potential for harm through implied judgments about student ability and teacher success. For writing ability, as with all performances, assessment must be displayed in detailed and specific verbal forms by an evaluator who is expert in the performance and who is experienced with the growth of the student being assessed. "Jessica's personal narrative includes a number of specific verbs—such as 'peppered,' 'tossed,' and 'mumbled'—that give her most recent piece a stronger voice than her earlier works" makes a contribution to the student that "Jessica scored a 162 on the NAEP 2002 writing exams, which is 2 points below the average for eighth-grade girls across the nation" does not and *cannot*.

Next, for teachers, most disturbing about the NAEP writing test is assessing the test itself; from a flawed writing test many valuable lessons can be garnered. First, do the writing prompts on the test reflect best practice in writing assignments, and do those prompts insure as much as possible that student performance on the essays reflects the student's ability to compose and not somehow other weaknesses in the student independent of writing ability (such as reading ability or cognitive development)? For instance, the writing prompt for grade 4 asks students to look at two surrealistic drawings and write a story (The PDF version of the prompts with student writing samples is available at http://nces.ed.gov). I am certain that the surrealistic drawing (coupled with the drawing requiring the student having certain cultural and social experiences and assumptions) and being asked to write fiction are both excellent reasons to discount all of the grade four data as accurate data about student writing ability *alone*; that prompt is flawed and almost insures that the writing sample is more a reflection of the child's cognitive development (and probably the child's culture) than the child's writing ability.

Further, the grade eight prompt requires the student to do a fairly significant amount of reading, thus tainting the data with the impact of student reading ability; the grade eleven prompt requires each student to have read and to be able to recall details about a favorite novel, and it claims to be asking for an informative essay, but the prompt reads: "Write an essay in which you discuss which book you would choose to save for future generations and *what it is about the book that makes it important to save* [emphasis added]." Isn't that a prompt for a persuasive essay? I am quite suspicious about NAEP's view of the essay intent and the rubric created to score the essays.

The questions raised above, along with the growing research concerning the negative impact standardized tests have on teaching and learning, show that we are at a crucial point concerning how educators and the general public will and should react to the stranglehold both politicians and the media have on education through the power of high-stakes testing. For instruction, the red flags are waving.

• • •

Though the observations made here concerning the inherent problems with standardized testing and the specific damage those tests inflict on writing instruction are out of step with the current call for high standards and educational accountability, I believe they offer an opportunity for teachers to reform instruction, for teachers to claim power over instruction—not at the command of tests such as the SAT or NAEP, but as a declaration of educational empowerment. If standardized tests fail ultimately in addressing the needs of our students and our schools, what should we now do in our pursuit of improved instruction? I suggest the following:

> • Immediately, call for legislation at the federal and state levels that insure that no standardized test stands as the sole factor for making any educational decision concerning a child or a school or a school system. Standardized test scores must be relegated to having only *a role* in policy and decisionmaking, not *the role*. We may allow that one-shot standardized tests, no matter how poor they are, stand as a trigger for addressing weaknesses in an individual student or groups of students, but we must demand that all final decisions about achievement be left in the hands of educators. People, not numbers, must oversee the fate of children.

> • Help create and implement assessment strategies that are authentic and that contribute to the political and social call for high standards and accountability (Brozo & Hargis, 2003). We have to concede some ground for traditional testing while we increase the role of authentic assessment of student work and ability.

> • Clearly define within our field, for students and parents (and for administrators, politicians, and the public) what matters in terms of learning and student performances of learning. Students acquiring any academic competence is a matter of *how* it is taught, not *if* it is taught.

> • Foster a broader community of expert instructors who practice their fields while infusing all teacher education programs with adequate and excellent preparation of teachers. Orga-

nized and widespread help for teachers to be experts in both their areas of content and in their teaching pedagogy is sadly missing. In its place stand standardized tests and political demands. That must change.

A call to reform classroom instruction is a valid one, one long overdue in any authentic and nonpoliticized form. But that call must come from the inside, from practicing instructors who are experts in their fields, not from the decisions made concerning standardized tests.

Counting on Assumptions of Classroom Teachers

If there is an American mind with its identifiable tendencies toward numbers as I describe in Chapter One, then certainly a teacher mind exists in classrooms across America. Many who have spent their lives teaching teachers have noticed that young and veteran teachers alike often revert in times of doubt and in times of high pressure to that which they know from their own lives as students; in other words, we often teach as we have been taught. Add to the mix that many educators at least survived, if not thrived, in traditional school settings where a number of misconceptions about learning and assessment have blossomed in the rich soil of behavioristic and positivistic assumptions. Try telling a group of undergrads planning to major in education that the SAT is a flawed instrument when most of those students have scored 1300 or above. "It worked for me!" they proclaim. We find it difficult to be skeptical about those things that *seem* true in our own unique experiences (Raymo, 1998).

The greatest threat to student learning when teachers (reflexively and without skepticism) teach as they have been taught is in the assumptions teachers bring to the classroom concerning learning and assessment. Most of those assumptions have been fed by our simplistic views of science and data gathering (as noted about the American psyche in general) and by the inordinate power standardized testing for the sake of labeling and judging has wielded over our students and teachers. The numbers games are not just played by politicians, pundits, and journalists; teachers in the classrooms play these games as well, directly with the children they hope to educate. These practices are daily reinforced in instruction and assessment as teachers are both encouraged and mandated to address high-stakes testing.

• • •

Here's the big dilemma: State and national testing are facts of our existence as educators; these assessments are often mandated by law, and they carry the weight of directing state and federal funds to our schools. As well, directly in the crosshairs of testing are both teachers and students. Jobs may be lost, students may be retained. So what does a right-minded teacher do in the face of institutionalized practices that go against everything that educator knows to be right and true in our profession?

Other than whining (we as teachers are good at that), let's be skeptical for a moment about some of the assumptions we have concerning numbers and quantifying in our classrooms; then we might find more alternatives than we first imagined, alternatives that would actually increase the rigor of our classes and enhance the learning of our students. Ideally, we will find that the new assumption is that best practice in instruction and assessment will coincidentally address those pitiful high-stakes tests even better than our current mindless conformity is producing.

The Bell-Shaped Curve Rings Loudly

The bell-shaped curve is a fact, isn't it? As the end of the 1800s drew near, America and the world slid faster and faster into the age of science. By the early and mid 1900s, numbers began to rule as the hallmark of science (supplanting the true heart of science, the scientific method), not just in daily commerce, but in the running of our schools. From time-on-task to the IQ test to the SAT and GPA, students more and more felt the weight of numbers. During this maelstrom, a statistical phenomenon, the bell-shaped curve, wedged its way firmly into the American psyche. And it remained there as a transparent assumption never to be questioned, equaled only as an assumption by behavioristic learning theory. Yet, many know that not only is the phenomenon debatable, but also it is a delicate fact to be applied.

The bell-shaped curve is a statistical phenomenon *describing* the distribution of empirical data drawn from a large population (the keys being "describing" and "large") although there is also a great deal of statistical comfort in applying the same concept in random samplings. As populations dwindle in size and as populations become skewed, the phenomenon disappears. Poof. But not for the average American and not for politicians with agendas easily served by the armor-plated truth of numbers.

If we place all humans on the planet on a distribution by height, then, yes, the numbers would form a neat bell-shaped curve with few who are quite short in adulthood, many who are similar in height (dominating the larger area around the epitome), and again a few who are quite tall. For educators, we must acknowledge that the bell-shaped curve describes well when we have a massive population (or a random sampling) and when we are measuring rather fixed phenomena such as height. When we have 17 learners in a classroom by coincidence of scheduling, or by choice of interest and ability, then the bell-shaped curve means nothing, notably because it describes. The bell-shaped curve does not predict in matters of performance: "Complex systems . . . are notoriously susceptible to chance," Raymo (1998) explains (p. 206).

The misconception of the bell-shaped curve leads teachers to *expect* that learning by a class will fall along a predictable curve within *any* class. Since classes are skewed populations and since learning is a demonstrably different thing than height, a teacher has absolutely no way to predict or expect any distribution of grades in a class. Virtually every combination of grades imaginable is possible depending on a huge array of factors; plotting the grade distribution after the course is complete is a somewhat valuable description of that class, but whether or not that distribution conforms to a bell-shaped curve means absolutely nothing.

This misconception can corrupt teaching and learning possibly worse than any other influence on learning in schools. If we inappropriately force any class or even the courses an individual teacher teaches to conform to a bell-shaped distribution, then we are forcing some students to fail arbitrarily. Further, most standardized testing is designed to force such a distribution of grades, again assuring that we will have failures. Teachers, the general public, and, most importantly, policy makers must embrace that learning is chaotic, idiosyncratic, and unpredictable. Grade distributions are of no value to public school teachers or the public if they are a false template within which we force all student performances; what administrators, teachers, parents, and students need to look at closely is the evidence available over a long period of time for each student. There they will find valuable data for enhancing that child's learning, that child's life.

Further, when schools group by ability as a policy (such as in public schools) or as a matter of course (the most academically able students tend to pursue college, while the nonacademic choose other avenues), then those subgroups certainly cannot and will not conform to a bell-shaped curve. But what educators ever explain to anyone that an Advanced Placement course of 12 students in a school of 950 students could quite easily have all A's because the students are excellent, both in ability and in motivation? It certainly should not have a bell-shaped distribution of scores; a teacher certainly should never force that class to fall along a bell-shaped distribution. In education, smaller, stratified populations are the rule, not the exception, so the bell-shaped curve means nothing in most student-teacher situations, at least in the actual classrooms faced by real teachers each day. Poof.

For classroom teachers, we must disregard entirely the predictability of grade distributions; they mean nothing from class to class, from year to year. If anything we can plot each set of grades along a distribution and say, "Well, that's how that class looks." Beyond that, plotting those scores means nothing.

Just Add the Grades and Do the Average, Dummy!

OK. I'll concede our tradition of giving students number and letter grades on assignments—though that can be refuted with solid arguments. But let's look at how educators tend without much reflection to bow to the act of averaging as if it were the only legitimate avenue for determining a child's future, as if averaging is by its nature fair or even accurate. Averaging has the allure of objectivity that haunts all that we do in schools, of course.

Remember the room of 10 people with a $140 among them? Now add this example about averages: Across town a patient enters a doctor's office to discover she has a temperature of 105° so she is immediately placed in a hospital. Over the course of a few days, after being prescribed antibiotics and given all the proper care, her chart shows a progression of temperature readings that is 105°, 105°, 104°, 102°, 102°, 100°, 98.6°. So the doctor adds the readings, divides by 7 and finds that the patient has at last reading an average temperature of just above 102°; Dr. Blue decides that the patient needs to stay in the hospital until her average is brought down to normal.

No! That didn't happen. Why? Medical doctors don't live in a world of averages as teachers do. The medical doctor is more concerned at any moment with the *current state of the patient*—a sense of the cumulative well-being of the patient.

"Hey!" I hear sophisticated quantitative evaluators yell. "The money example is flawed because the population is too small." Valid argument. (Yes, one I used to refute the sacred bell-shaped curve). So let's increase the population. The average family in the U.S. has 2.4 children (or some such number). The population such a number is drawn from is huge, in the millions. But compare the statistical truth of 2.4 with reality. In reality *there is no living, breathing average family since there is no .4 child.* Again, statistical truth clashes with reality. Despite the size of the population, an average is always a distortion of the reality it attempts to describe. Averaging also assumes that the average status is more important than the ultimate status, a terribly flawed perception in relation to learning.

The problem here is the assumptions that swirl around our slavery to numbers. Few teachers ever even consider the broad range of statistical possibilities such as mean, median, and mode, much less the possibility of assigning numerical or letter grades based on the whole of ones professional judgment. What if a student scored over a grading period these grades: 10, 10, 85, 85, 85, 85, 85, 85, 100, 100? The average that most teachers would assign is 73. But doesn't the data also suggest that 85 might be a more accurate reflection of the child's ability? The 10s and 100s seem to be aberrations, while the median and mode might reflect more accurately the true ability of the student. Or what if a student scored those grades in that order? Might not the final 100 show a cumulative level of knowledge and understanding and suggest the child deserves a 100 for a final grade, especially if that final test were designed to be a cumulative assessment? The approach to determining a final grade is highly complex and relative to the student, the purposes of the grading, and the form and intent of the assessments themselves.

The cult of averaging is a classroom version of the standardized test phenomenon we have explored earlier. Averaging grades is a longstanding tradition that parents, teachers, administrators, and even students will never question (again, it reeks of objectivity and shall never be touched); the mathematical average is an easy thing to hide behind if a teacher wishes to relinquish his authority, if a teacher wishes to avoid confrontation over things that matter. It's how we do things. It seems fair because of the momentum of tradition. In the reality of the classroom and in the context of assessment and grades existing to support learning, the mystique of averaging fades much as the certainty of the bell-shaped curve dissipates.

Numerical grades on student assessments are best used as one set of markers for the professional decisions that educators must make from child to child at each grading period. Averaging a set of grades over a grading period to compare that with other evaluations of that data and of the student's performances is perfectly legitimate, but using "that's his average" as a scapegoat for professional evaluations of students is reprehensible and a clear distortion of the reality of that student's ability and achievement, much like our refrain of "It's on the test."

He's a "C" Student, and She's a Solid "A-"

Even the NFL has a number that is a descriptor of a quarterback's ability. And college football uses a complex and computer-driven system of stats to determine what teams are best. In our most frivolous distractions in America we have let actual sport, the playing of the games, be overrun with numbers.

And this has been the case in our most precious field as well, education. We try to be clever and substitute capital letters for numbers (As, Bs, Cs, Ds, and Fs—and I worked for years where we even assigned Es in that system for the barely failing, but failing nonetheless), but assigning numbers as descriptors is firmly entrenched in education. And this practice determines children's lives.

Giving grades—now more than ever, *that* means numbers and not letters—is a reductionistic system at best and misleading at worst. During my 18 years of teaching, I saw daily that two students with the same grades were as different from each other as two students separated by two or three letter grades. For instance, I often had students making identical 94 averages, then portrayed as an A-. Yet there are two distinct A- students—one who works like hell, but has limited ability, and one who is quite able, but does the bare minimum of that student's ability in the context of the expectations for the class. That description I wrote to characterize these two hypothetical students is more accurate than any A-. Teachers who have daily contact with the work and the students who produce that work see those distinctions clearly, but are willing to allow the current system to blur those distinctions for the tradition of assigning single final grades to primarily label and even sort students.

Reducing humans to numbers, whether it is a social security or driver's license number, or an SAT score or GPA, is a dehumanizing part of the modern world. Yes, I admit that much of this is necessary, but I also contend that we can do a much better job, especially in education.

It's Rank to Be Ranked

Now, we again turn to that trusted friend, the SAT. Why? Because that number has burrowed its way into the very fiber of existence for almost all people, whether college is in their future or not. It determines college entrance (so they say), it determines college scholarships, and, most importantly, it falsely marks the quality of the state's schools where our children learn.

I happen to live in a bottom-feeder state, one where everyone (the pro-education and anti-education folk alike) laments that we are either 49th or 50th in the nation in education. The source of such a proclamation? Ranking states by average SAT scores. And what happens when you try to explain that the ranking is inaccurate? You are labeled an incompetent educrat who wants to pad his pockets with taxpayer money. Pulling aside the political baggage surrounding the SAT, let's look at the largest danger empirical data pose for education, the proclivity to rank.

An impressive array of educational researchers and evaluators has begun to speak out over the last decade about educational testing and the numbers games. They have shown essentially that educational testing that produces statistical data is a complex system fraught with complex problems. In short, standardized tests must be designed to gather inauthentic work in academic settings (as opposed to authentic performances of understanding); that is the nature of large-scale, selected-response testing. Further, those tests are guided by complex principles of evaluation—reliability, validity, and norms and such. The tests themselves are designed to insure the assumptions of quantification, notably bell-shaped curves, thus forcing a distribution of scores that appears to rank from failure to excellence.

Beyond the inherent self-fulfilling nature of standardized testing, the data culled from such tests create an even more evil monster, the ability to rank. Again, the SAT. Throughout my professional career, The College Board has released SAT data, including state-by-state listings of average SAT scores. That table clearly explains that ranking of states by SAT scores is inappropriate; they have even turned to listing the states alphabetically to help fight the urge to rank. But every year the media ranks. As it ranks everything else.

Larger than the debate over the SAT is the penchant for ranking in the empirical world, especially in education. Two issues refute such rankings—comparing vastly differing populations and the statistical gaps among those being ranked. I have touched on apples and oranges before, but nowhere is such a discrepancy seen as with ranking by average SAT scores. In my home state of South Carolina, over the last decade we have about 50% to 60% of eligible students taking the SAT; within that group only about 25% of those students have taken the college-prep courses recommended by The College Board. In its totality, this data help us see that SAT scores in SC are likely to reflect primarily *the coursework taken by students* (along with socioeconomic and family factors that we'll ignore for now); in other words, students who take college-prep courses do better on an exam intended to measure college success than students who do not take college-prep courses. Hmm. Yet the state is yearly compared to states where only 6% or 8% of students take the SAT with all of those students having taken the college-prep courses recommended by The College Board. Isn't it fair to suggest that SAT ranking by states is unfair?

An additional danger of ranking, since rankings are often displayed without the data creating the ranking, is the comparison between the range of differences among the scores and the margin of error of the study. It is common for rankings showing a spread of information from 1 through 20 to use data so finely delineated that in reality all 20 are statistically the same (Bracey, 1997a). Even more disturbing is that often ties in those rankings will be listed alphabetically, making the national standing in the world dependent on whether we are listed as "America" or the "United States." Journalists love rankings, just as Americans love numbers, because numbers don't lie, and, well, we want only to be Number One.

Giving Them What They Want—Reporting Grades

We *have* to put spelling grades on the report cards so we *have* to give spelling tests. Right? Well, no. As with Warner (1993) recognizing that English teachers often persist in questionable instructional and assessment strategies because of the threat of standardized tests, classroom teachers often fall into teaching and testing traps because of the least important reasons, the bureaucracy of reporting grades.

A common cause of isolated skills instruction is that teachers are required to post isolated grades—report card spaces for spelling, for instance. Again, teachers often revert to traditional approaches without considering that isolated grades may be pulled from holistic performances. In a graduate course on adolescent literature, I actually had a teacher say that she *had* to give spelling tests because a spelling grade *had* to go on district-mandated report cards (though she was quick to admit that her experience as a teacher had shown that spelling tests did not improve her students' ability to spell in authentic activities, such as their own writing).

Should the nature of grade reporting dictate our classroom practices? We have known for decades that isolated instruction and assessment of literacy skills—phonics, spelling, vocabulary, grammar, etc.—are *not* best practice; all of the components that constitute literacy are best learned in holistic and authentic ways. And spelling lists that lead to spelling tests each week are *not* how we foster good spellers. Spelling grades would serve students and teachers best if the grades were pulled from authentic writing assignments completed by students who were aware that any particular piece would be graded specifically for spelling ability.

At least in Tennessee, and probably in most states, the reporting of grades, the report card, is being reformatted to reflect the state standards (Long, 2003). This will insure that teacher behavior is impacted since parents are being notified regularly how their students are performing *in relationship to the standards*. Again, the danger is that teacher practices and parental perceptions are at the command of the standards, which prove again and again to be reductionistic, which prove to hurt more than they help when we are concerned about student learning for understanding.

Isolated displays of student achievement should not dictate how we teach and how we test in our classrooms. If a district or parents demand isolated grades for spelling, vocabulary, or grammar, then we can provide those through best practice until we teach *them* that such isolated grades mean little when compared to authentic assessments of student performances over a long period of time.

The Dangers of Quantifying—Fearing the Rubric

Rubrics are the authentic solution to grading student performances;
we must add them to our best practice arsenal. Sorry. Maybe not. In
the political dynamic of testing and more testing, rubrics for teaching
and assessment have emerged as the strongest contribution made by
educators concerned with student performances and authentic assessment. Simply put, a rubric offers a more complex and often ex-
pository explanation of student behaviors in very specific terms, so
the evaluation is more fully explained for the learner and the teacher,
both during instruction and after the assessment. We should tell students what their performances should look like if they are going to be
held accountable, the philosophy of rubrics contends.

The specific and descriptive nature of rubrics combined with the
intent of rubric-driven assessment to support instruction and learning
makes the rubric hard to discount. But rubrics have been co-opted by
the standardized testing movement and by the high-standards police.
The result has been that rubrics *of a certain type* have become ammu-
nition to impose learning, which I would characterize as indoctrination, not learning for understanding. Mabry (1999) and Hillocks
(2003) provide serious warnings that rubric-driven standardized assessment of student performances restricts and corrupts student
learning for understanding as negatively as selected-response assessment.

In a time of accountability, it seems *safe* and even smart to clearly
design the ends of instruction (show exactly what is expected) so
teachers know what to encourage, so students know what to do. Design the goal first, then make it happen. Rubrics fit neatly into that
paradigm. But that is not education; at least it is not education in a
free society, it is not education where the humanity of children is
prized above all else.

This caution about rubrics means that we must be sure to implement rubrics that support learning for students and that encourage
performances of understanding by students; such rubrics can be designed, but teachers and the public must be cautioned that rubrics
come in many forms, some good and some bad. Again, the rubric as a
part of assessment that supports student learning is a wonderful
thing, but as soon as the rubric becomes a device of prescription to
facilitate standardized assessment, we lose any advantage that a rubric may offer.

The Reasons for Grading

What does a grade mean after all? This is a key question every teacher should face. A grade on an assignment that cannot be attempted again is much different than a grade on work intended to be re-worked. A grade on an individual assignment is not the same as a grade assigned for a fixed grading period, either.

Grading assignments needs to be directly addressed by teachers, preferably in conjunction with students and their parents. The assigning of grades is a relative thing. Teachers, students, and parents need to be reeducated that the primary purpose of grades is to support learning by the student (Egan, 2003). The ultimate use of grades to label and judge students is a necessary evil that should be left to the inevitability of fixed grading periods.

In my own classes, to change the attitudes of students concerning grades, I often give checks on assignments, especially the large number of assignments that are designed to be both the assessment and a learning experience in and of themselves (though that learning is unpredictable and varied from student to student, and that is OK). Students and parents invariably want to know "How will checks be averaged?" I always say, "As a check." Not a very satisfying answer since a check is not a number. Eventually, I simply reeducate my students to react differently to being assessed; they could get a check or a zero on those assignments. The power of the zero, a number that isn't a number, eventually allays their questions; students embrace the check-ness of the check out of a desire *not* to receive the dreaded zero that *could* be averaged (even when I stopped averaging grades, I was unable to stop students from referring to "averaging" to reach their final grades). Sometimes we should simply get credit for the experience, and numbers will not do.

To free classrooms from the tyranny of numbers, teachers must create a climate of assessment that supports learning. The classroom cannot remain a slave to mirroring standardized tests at the expense of student understanding and at the expense of the dignity of children.

To that end, classrooms might thrive best if teachers work toward narrative and verbal forms of assessment. During the 1930s, LaBrant (Thomas, 2001) and the other progressive educators implemented narrative report cards at the University School of OSU while participating in the Eight-Year Study, and research many years later showed that those students did as well if not better than students suffering the slings and arrows of letter and number grades.

Does Any Question Really Matter?

Teacher and institutional assumptions about testing, grounded as they are in a misconception about the bell-shaped curve, have created other weaknesses in classroom assessments concerning, again, content. Teachers often function under conflicting pressures—the institutional demands for grade distributions running up against most teachers' compassion, their desire to see all students succeed. The result is the arbitrary and simplistic nature of selected-response testing in classrooms.

In most settings, some arbitrary percentage is the mark for passing, often 70 % at the public school level. Nonetheless, that percentage is arbitrary. Further, each student in the class may answer correctly *any* combination of 70% of the questions and pass. In reality, then, no single question on the test is essential, though most testing of this kind is based on the premise that some body of content is essential. Unconsciously (I would argue), many teachers believe that students are limited by IQ (another troubling number) so the tests often contain a significant amount of pure knowledge (since our simplistic conception of Bloom's Taxonomy of Cognition suggests knowledge to be something we might call "easy"), at least enough easy material that any student who tries might pass.

What a mess.

Assumptions and arbitrary markers of passing make the neat number we garner from a test seem much less certain than "90 is a B." Number gathering through objective, content-based tests for the good old report card is a messy thing.

The Onus of Being Labeled Smart—Or Not

And what about IQ? Measuring the potential humans have for intelligence is a precarious adventure—fraught with what we mean by intelligence, how we measure intelligence, and whether or not we believe that the potential for learning is fixed at birth. Regardless of the debates swirling around IQ, what a teacher believes about IQ, or just each child's potential for learning, affects profoundly the teaching and learning in that class.

Howard Gardner (1999b) has at least dented educators' faith in and misconceptions about intelligence; the popular perception, I would argue, has been left unscathed. Alfred Binet, Gardner notes, offered a seminal attempt to measure intelligence in France during the early 1900s:

> From Binet's time on, intelligence tests have been heavily weighted toward measuring verbal memory, verbal reasoning, numerical reasoning, appreciation of logical sequences, and ability to state how one would solve problems of daily living. (p. 12)

For most in contemporary society, lay people and professional educators, IQ is a verifiable and measurable fact: "[B]y the mid-1920s, the intelligence test had become a fixture in educational practice in the United States" (Gardner, 1999b, p. 13). More disturbing yet may be that we have not only allowed our perceptions of intelligence to become fixed and narrow, but also allowed the tests of intelligence to dictate what counts as intelligence: "[T]he influential Harvard psychologist E. G. Boring declared, 'Intelligence *is* what the tests test'" (Gardner, 1999b, p. 13).

That bell-shaped curve raises its ugly head again here. The popular perception of IQ, one shared by most teachers, is that IQ is fixed at birth and that IQ falls along a bell-shaped curve distribution for all humanity. In the classroom, that means that it is expected and acceptable for some students to have low achievement, for teachers to ask very little of some students because *a percentage of humans just are not capable of excelling*, they believe. Standardized testing only exacerbates these conceptions since they are designed to insure such distributions of grades and they correlate strongly with IQ measurements (Gould, 1996).

Possibly the most complete discussion of IQ and the hazards connected with quantifying intelligence and committing to "the theory of a measurable, genetically fixed, and unitary intelligence" is *The Mismeasure of Man* (Gould, 1996, p. 21). Inspired by Charles Darwin's fear of the dehumanization of people by institutions, particularly through the power of science, Gould provides a solid argument that quantifying intelligence is a messy thing, that normal distributions (the bell-shaped curve) are suspect, and that America has perverted Binet's attempt to measure intelligence; in short, he adds: "[T]he entire con-

cept of IQ as a unitary biological property becomes nonsense" when
we explore it in all its complexities (p. 22). His discussion of IQ also
supports some of the earlier generalizations made here. The American
fascination with, trust in, and manipulation of IQ is but one example
of tendencies to reduce the complex to the simple, to present the abstract in concrete ways, to simplify spectrums into either/or dualities,
and to rank (Gould, p. 27).

Further, Gould (1996) explains that IQ as we see it today is a pe-
culiarly American thing and a distortion from Binet's original intent
for measuring intelligence. H. H. Goddard made IQ popular in the
U.S., claims Gould, but Lewis M. Terman played the greatest role:
"Goddard introduced Binet's scale to America, but Terman was the
primary architect of its popularity" (p. 205). From Terman's work, the
Stanford-Binet test became the crux of all intelligence testing in
America; Gould explains that correlating IQ tests with the Stanford-
Binet test became more important than questioning whether or not IQ
could be measured at all. The result has been that "[t]hirty minutes
and five tests [would] mark a child for life" when schools jumped on
the IQ bandwagon as a means for labeling the potential in children to
learn (p. 207). IQ is a powerful number, and it lurks in every corner of
the classrooms across the U. S.

Numbers such as IQ or test scores more often than not conspire to
lower teacher expectations for students, to insure failure. When we
set aside these assumptions as teachers and teach each child as a human with unpredictable potential, then our schools might perform at
a level we could have never planned.

Starting from Nothing—Of Zero and One Hundred

And then there are tasks concerning grading that teachers perform
that seem quite harmless on the surface. Most teachers begin the actual marking of assessment and assigning of grades by subtracting
missed points from 100 to calculate a student's grade. This raises several problems.

First, subtracting from 100 suggests that students begin with a
100% *without ever doing anything*. In reality, students begin all assessments at 0% since they have not done anything. Next, marking the
incorrect and subtracting to tally a grade reinforces for students the
need to avoid errors. Avoiding mistakes is one of the great weak-

nesses of behavioristic learning theory; in constructivistic learning theory, we embrace the need to make errors in order to learn.

Starting all students with a 100 and subtracting points sends messages to students that are countereducational. By switching the grading of assessment to giving students credit for what they do well, a teacher can create a climate conducive to using assessment to support student learning, instead of reducing testing to labeling and punishing students for their weaknesses.

Objecting to the Behavioral Objective—It Must Be Measurable

Numbers are often at the center of a belief in the need for structure, the need for control. Traditional planning still dominates how teachers approach teaching and assessment. That planning is behavioristic in nature, imposing a prescribed content. Assessment is also driven by those behavioral objectives that must be observable and *measurable*. Things of the heart and the soul have no place in our lesson plans or our tests, thus our schools.

The current standards and accountability movement bolstered by NCLB has increased the likelihood that teachers are required to plan meticulously and well into the future. Pacing guides and benchmark tests monitor that teachers remain on task while those same teachers monitor that their own students remain on task. The twin beasts of coverage and quantification are fed daily by teachers conforming to a reductionistic view of planning, thus instruction and assessment.

Traditional planning has been revitalized, and teachers seem not only hesitant to challenge such planning but also eager to embrace that structure. Again, this planning is flawed if we want students to learn for understanding, if we want both teachers and students empowered within the institution we called public education.

• • •

Our schools are under an unprecedented federal assault to standardize public education, but research is revealing that even mandated standards and high-stakes standards cannot insure any sort of consistent standards from state to state, despite the power of federal dollars. When state standards are compared they are drastically different; many students could improve their status simply by moving to a different state (Hammond, 2003); as well, those high-stakes tests offer little evidence of college success (Cavanagh, 2003).

The pressure is high, but schools are struggling with standardizing assessment; many are questioning if such standardization can be done, if such standardization is even desirable (Strauss, 2003). As well, the tests themselves are failing (Henriques, 2003). The results we are most certain about are the negative impacts that accountability, high standards, and high-stakes testing are having on teachers and students. As I stated in the beginning of this chapter, mandates do not insure that classroom practices are what we think they are; Kauffman, Johnson, Kardos, Liu, and Peske (2002) have found that today's federal and state mandates have not translated into new teachers knowing what they are supposed to be doing from day to day in their classes. The result is they are leaving the profession feeling overburdened and underprepared. This study seems to suggest that we are at a paradoxical moment in education when teachers long for guidance at the same time that leaders in education criticize the standards movement for being too prescriptive, thus mandating the life out of the field of teaching.

If we save public education (more about the threat in Chapter Four), we must immediately work to improve that system, since this current political climate has created a mess that does stir up a great deal of problems that we can address well. The classroom is where the changes must begin; the source of that change will be each teacher. Again, numbers matter very little; people matter more than we can ever measure.

• • •

Miller (1999), in his discussion of evolutionary theory and natural selection, offers an interesting analogy: Our schools function as natural selection does, with test-taking abilities as key factors in weeding out the fittest for college (pp. 13–14). This seems to be an apt but frightening comparison; those numbers from testing work to determine access to knowledge for America's children. In the classrooms across our democracy, we serve those children better and our society better if we change the parameters for determining the fittest—determining who gains access to knowledge, thus individual empowerment.

FOUR

Dismantling Public
Education by the Numbers

Paulo Freire (1993) warns, "One of the basic elements of the relationship between oppressor and oppressed is *prescription*" (p. 28). In effect, mandates by those in power dictate what is true, what is right, what counts. In this discussion so far, I have been exploring the impact assumptions, beliefs, and misconceptions about numbers and science have on the educating of children in our public schools. Here, we will begin to look more closely at NCLB as one of those potentially oppressive prescriptions Freire identifies—a prescription made more dangerous since it directly affects literacy instruction across the U.S., since it often masks itself in addressing the educational needs of the impoverished—and consider the threat such mandates pose for public education as a vital institution in a democracy. As well, I will look closely at the need to improve literacy education for the impoverished as a contrast to the *prescribed* and flawed approaches within NCLB and the school choice initiatives that often claim to be primarily concerned with the needs of the poor. NCLB and calls for school choice or the privatization of schooling may be a greater threat to the democracy we call America than most would admit.

• • •

Michael Winerip (2003) attended an American Educational Research Association (AERA) conference and concluded: "I got the impression that in education research, most anything that is provable is also disprovable." This observation might be clever and somewhat innocuous if we were not in the grips of NCLB and if the federal gov-

ernment were not spending money simply to promote federal legislation, an agenda that appears to insure the end of public education in
America (Davis, 2003).

In NCLB, a presidential administration has codified through legislation a certain type of empirical research, as if nothing else can or
does exist. Briefly, reading instruction in America is now governed by
research, which sounds logical. But the law has identified that *only*
empirical studies can be referenced. Again, what's so wrong with
that? If the discussions in earlier chapters have not been enough to
call quantification into question, let's look at the cycle that will harm
students learning to read in this 2004 America. Then, we can begin to
suspect, if not prove, that NCLB and the entire standards and high-
stakes testing movement is poised to discredit public schools and
public school teachers so Americans will choose school choice and in
effect dismantle public education. Money is to be made in our schools
and in place of our schools.

As noted above, empirical data drawn from standardized testing
has clear parameters, rigid paradigms, and issues of implementation
that dictate addressing skills in isolation. For reading this means that
empirical studies tend to test isolated reading skills such as phonemic
awareness and tend to put students in artificial settings dealing with
carefully selected texts (ones best suited for testing) and carefully
crafted questions that deal with clearly delineated reading skills (remember the warning earlier about the self-fulfilling nature of standardized testing and recall the flaws inherent in the NAEP testing of
writing in 2002). Now, what does all this mean?

Since empirical studies must function within isolated and inauthentic assessment situations, student performance on such tests can
often be enhanced by instruction that is isolated and inauthentic. So?
What's wrong with that? If one is not expert in the field of literacy,
this all sounds good, manageable and effective. But the great body of
evidence over a decade of modern education and linguistics study
shows that students learn to read best through holistic and authentic
instruction. American slavery to empirical data has created a political
system that steamrolls best practice in instruction for student
achievement to get to numbers. The quantitative world is neater, it is
more manageable, and the charts are cool.

The qualitative world, on the other hand, is chaotic and idiosyncratic, and who wants to read paragraph after paragraph describing
complex phenomena? Especially in the morning paper when there are

so many neat charts. This brings us to the ultimate crux of this discussion: America and its schools function in two distinct realities, the reality of numbers and the reality of re-creation. And the uncomfortable truths are that numbers don't lie, but they do, and that case studies, biographies, and narratives don't lie, but they do.

The solution? We need equal footings for the quantitative world and the qualitative nature of educational research, each working to enhance and inform the other. And each world needs its supporters and its skeptics, maybe the skeptics more than anything. Then we need to join hands and face the country as a whole, especially in terms of literacy education and especially as that impacts the most disenfranchised members of our society—children living in poverty, children born to a language other than English.

• • •

Johnny can't read? Well, maybe and maybe not. What do you mean by "read"? Maybe Johnny was born into a home of low socio-economic status where the parents were undereducated and where literacy opportunities were low or nonexistent. After entering school, Johnny may have performed low on the readiness exam. Since his first weeks of school, Johnny may have been in low-level courses doing thousands of worksheets to prepare him for state testing—that he fails and fails and fails. Maybe Johnny can't read because he has never been allowed to read, never been engaged as a reader—having spent his academic career labeled "slow" or "underachiever" and expected only to fill in the blanks. But Johnny is way more than his below-standard 684 score on the verbal section of the high school exit exam. Johnny is a hell of a lot more than that number if only someone would look closely and carefully at that life instead of quantifying it.

The Politics of How We Teach—NCLB as Assault on Academia

Over the past 20-odd years, the most current educational reform movements have gained a cyclic momentum—the early 1980s reform wave cresting before dissipating on the beach, then followed immediately by a larger and more erosive wave of reform known as NCLB. From governors to presidents, political leaders of every party have rushed to be our Education Governor or Education President in recent decades. Whether it is Richard Riley in SC or Ronald Reagan proclaiming *A Nation at Risk* or Bill Clinton, fist raised, promising "all third graders will read," politicians have discovered political capital in the condemnation of public schools, from prekindergarten to graduate school, as we have explored throughout this discussion. Our schools, it seems, are the source of all of America's ills from a floundering economy to the rise of reality TV.

Since the early 1980s, we have witnessed an evolution in the necessary marriage between politics and education—where education available to all is funded by taxes pooled for the social welfare in an avowedly capitalistic society leery of socialistic endeavors, a people who have superficial and baffling perceptions of numbers and science. Politicians own a bully pulpit concerning education because of their elected positions, not because they have any expertise in running schools. If we look closely, in fact, those governors and presidents, and our state superintendents of education, have either no (in most cases) or very little experience or education as educators themselves. The history of American education over the past 100 years has seen this drama unfold in slightly differing degrees virtually nonstop, but recent efforts by the George W. Bush administration should make everyone in the academic community, not just those in public education, pause and assess both the direct and the subtle threats leveled by NCLB at academia, at public schools, and at our democracy.

• • •

As I have noted earlier, I made the observation in the late 1990s that politicians could gain political power through manipulating the accountability of schools (Thomas, 1999). I would add now, just 5 years later, that this is exactly what the Bush administration has done in NCLB, with "scientific research" and "high standards" as its mantra. Bush's home state of Texas has already begun experimenting with scripted curriculum that dictates everything spoken by teachers and deemed acceptable from students—all driven of course by the state assessment (TAAS, in its first manifestation) and, tacitly, the state standards.

Although NCLB has garnered a high profile in the media, particularly in the print media, most who have been following the initiative would probably associate it solely with public schools, and many would initially support concepts such as "high standards," "scientifically based reform," and "highly qualified teachers." When the sound bites and doublespeak are pushed aside, though, a political and ideological intent becomes apparent, an intent that may be unprecedented in its direct assault by conservative ideologues on academia.

NCLB covers a staggering number of topics, including school prayer (ESEA/NCLB Analysis, 2003) and other social/educational issues reflected 2 decades earlier in Reagan's educational plans. A few key issues, though, unmask the political and cultural agenda that is at the heart of the NCLB legislation, some of which I have touched on earlier:

• NCLB mandates reading instruction and comes precipitously close to endorsing a single reading program (Open Court by McGraw-Hill, which conducted internal research to support its program with claimed "scientific" evidence) that would insure huge revenues for the publishing company.

• NCLB overtly challenges the existence of colleges of education, endorsing alternative avenues to teacher certification and the eradication of colleges of education; Texas, Bush's home political state, has shown a strong move to offer alternative certification for teachers that sends a clear message: "'It says that teachers are not professionals—that anybody can do it'" (Galley, 2003).

• NCLB increases public schools' dependence on the federal government for funding; also NCLB helps reinforce the use of high-stakes tests as the sole determinants of student credit for a complete course or high school graduation.

• NCLB mandates *what* research is legitimate, exclusively accepting only narrow forms of experimental and quasi-experimental studies that NCLB also misrepresents and manipulates to advance a particular ideological agenda (while excluding decades of valuable qualitative data).

• • •

At the turn of the 20th century, the industrialization and modernization of the U.S. economy seemingly necessitated longer and more effective education for American citizens. Concurrent with the industrialization came the scientific explosion; business learned that a certain type of measuring and quantifying helped make production more efficient, thus more profitable. This move to increase efficiency was soon superimposed onto schools. Modern society needed better-educated students, and the profit success of efficiency models in industry suggested that the same business model would improve schools (Berliner & Biddle, 1995, pp. 139–144; Bracey, 1997a; Ringer & Bineham, 1995). Free market ideology evolved into a free market metaphor that became the default panacea for any system in America (Ringer & Bineham, 1995).

Yet, by WWII, America learned through IQ and literacy tests given to soldiers that illiteracy and semiliteracy appeared to be alarmingly high among the troops, even after decades of modeling schools on the business model. The political response, a conservative response to educational reform that is consistent throughout the past 6 or 7 decades, was to blame erroneously progressive and liberal education for the failure of schools. In fact, schools were better than ever (Moore & Simon, 2000), and the soldiers had overwhelmingly attended traditional schools patterned on the efficiency model. Nonetheless, political mandates called for higher standards and greater measurement, again.

With the launching of Sputnik in 1957 by the Soviets, America and its political leaders once again cried foul; schools in America were surely failing. On the heels of our apparent loss in the space race, teacher-proof curriculum was developed and (yes, again) standards were raised and measurements increased. This third major decry against mediocre American education was followed 2 decades later by *A Nation at Risk*—which made yet another careless political assault on public education and spawned the Goals 2000 initiative (or Educate America Act), embraced by governors and presidents on both the Left and the Right.

Today, we are under the most recent manifestation of this political cycle. It is important to realize that the cycle is flawed and persistent, but it is probably more important to identify the driving forces behind NCLB. Like the political and social criticisms of schools in the past, NCLB has several key arguments and assumptions at its core:

- Schools are failing America, and this imperils economic survival and dominance.

- Education is too often theory and ideology driven at the expense of research.

- Public education is essentially flawed since it is a socialistic entity; it exists outside the market metaphor, so it is corrupt.

• The future success of our democracy and our capitalistic economy depends on highly educated students who are properly trained to enter the work-force.

• Market ideology is a panacea for any failed system.

• Educators must be policed from the outside, as a duty to taxpayers, since professionals inside a system *not* based on the competition model cannot be trusted.

While most of these assumptions are refutable, it is only fair to point out that educational reform movements are often initiated by people with good intent; that said, good intent is not enough, especially when the good intent is corrupted by a lack of expertise in the field and shaded by a blind allegiance to a political and cultural ideology—and ultimately based on false assumptions and many misconceptions about science and research, the numbers that run our society.

• • •

Before we explore the specific assaults leveled by NCLB, we need to look at the larger picture of federal and state mandates concerning education, especially in the context of the avowed posture of the political conservatives who support local control whenever possible. During the conservative political revolution of the 1980s, *A Nation at Risk* sounded a call to help the failing public schools in America. The poorly informed and politically manipulated public has believed these broad condemnations of American schools each generation, also blindly accepting that in some distant and romanticized past ideal schools existed (although at any point in that past schools were being resoundingly condemned).

A strong case can and has been made concerning the flaws with both the political and public conclusions drawn from *A Nation at Risk*. As noted earlier, in short, "the report was a veritable treasury of slanted, spun, and distorted statistics" (Bracey, 2003a, p. 617). Thus, a dynamic was established in the early 1980s of manipulating scientific and statistical data to give political ideology a veneer of gravity. This eventually metamorphosed into NCLB.

During the Reagan years, conservatives made grassroots efforts to influence education by running for school boards and influencing text adoptions in the schools, reflecting a local-control philosophy that seems consistent with contemporary conservative ideology. While the conservative influence at the school-board level fluctuated for a good 20 years, the impact is hard to measure. Yet, during that same time, states did initiate and develop standards and testing initiatives that have grown, with little to abate them; additionally, over that time, the drive for high standards and accountability have spurred the high-stakes testing boom that consists almost exclusively of selected-response testing. The market metaphor and standards movement had already taken strong root in public education well before NCLB, providing a solid base for the Bush initiative.

With NCLB, though, a new twist has been added—direct and powerful federal control and mandates for not only public education but also academia as a whole. Manzo and Hoff (2003) explain that while NCLB appears to limit federal control of educational policy, it actually greatly increases Washington's power over local schools in America. When the standards movement blossomed in the 1980s, primarily as a phenomenon of state government, little resistance manifested itself; with the growth at the federal level, though, many from journalists to parents and students have begun to grow skeptical. Bob Herbert (2003) acknowledges a "War on Schools" in *The New York Times*, and even a 15-year-old in Florida has mounted a revolt against high-stakes testing (Fischer, 2003), reflecting that many are increasingly coming to see through the veneer of "high standards" and the power of numbers to the negative impact political initiatives have on student learning.

NCLB represents a federal mandate not just of high standards for students and teachers, but *how* those standards may be measured and *what* and *how* teachers teach in their classrooms. Further, this legislation gives the federal government authority over many areas of academia that belong within the academic debate, not at the whim of political mandates, such as how teachers should be taught and certified, what counts as legitimate research, and whether education should be standardized and mandated from a centralized power.

• • •

The war over teaching reading has been a long and mostly unproductive one, stretching back to the 1920s and 1930s when research began supporting holistic methodologies over isolated instruction. Each time the argument is raised, sides are chosen, such as "whole language versus phonics." With NCLB, the rhetoric and reductionistic nature of the debate is nothing new, regretfully. While I will not belabor the point here, the reading debate as framed above is a false debate (one designed to provide cover for ideological agendas) since the argument properly stated is not about *what* reading teachers should teach (as in whether or not to address phonemic awareness) but about *how* to teach reading; the *what* debate is pointless (we know and have known for decades what characteristics fluent readers exhibit), but the *how* debate is productive and necessary. NCLB attempts to settle the *what* debate, falsely, and eradicates the *how* debate entirely (Zimmermann & Brown, 2003).

NCLB mandates that all reading instruction should be phonics-based and all reading programs must show scientific research supporting the program in order to qualify for federal funding. From Gerald Coles (2003), Regie Routman (2003), Joanne Yatvin (2002, 2003), Stephen Krashen (2002a, 2002b), and a whole host of experts in reading and research, we have ample evidence to raise the following concerns about NCLB and its reading mandates:

• The National Reading Panel (NRP) began with a clearly defined agenda and selected research to conform to that agenda, thus practicing specious science themselves.

• The research and science behind NCLB and the tacitly endorsed Open Court reading program are flawed and tainted by self-interests and cooked data (Coles, 2003; Coles, 2000, pp. 31–42; Routman, 2003, pp. 189–191, 196–198; Camilli, Vargas, & Yurecko, 2003).

• Decades of research support reading instruction best practice (Zemelman, Daniels, & Hyde, 1998) are discounted through questionable conclusions drawn about research in general in the NCLB mandates.

• Selected-response assessments that test reading skills in isolation are driving reading instruction at the expense of educationally sound goals such as reading comprehension and methods such as authentic assessment.

Reading mandates in NCLB reveal the dangers in ideologically motivated policy in education. Further, the NRP represents a contemporary precedent that must be challenged, agenda-driven policy that both dictates and manipulates academic and scientific pursuits.

NCLB reading legislation creates a vicious cycle: Isolated phonics instruction is easily tested in standardized, selected-response formats; thus, if the powers that be can establish phonemic awareness as *equal to* reading in the public mind, then the teaching of reading can be mandated, tested, and documented as improving through seemingly scientific data, with political gain waiting at the end of the process for those who mandate—although the students themselves will likely be able only to read the report aloud, not understanding a word of it.

• • •

Rod Paige (2002), in his annual report on teacher quality, clearly states that NCLB intends to create highly qualified teachers. The report concludes that effective teaching depends on verbal skills and content knowledge, not pedagogy; in other words, no one needs any direct instruction in how to teach. NCLB directly discounts both state departments of education and colleges of education as unneeded: "States' systems [of teacher certification] seem to maintain low standards and high barriers at the same time," the Executive Summary proclaims (p. vii). Ironically, NCLB attacks both of these entities as costly bureaucratic excesses while simultaneously establishing unprecedented federal bureaucracy with the legislation and ideological strings attached to abundant federal money.

Yet, the Association for Supervision and Curriculum Development ("Research-Based Characteristics of High-Quality Teacher Preparation," 2003), Cochran-Smith and Fries (2001), and Darling-Hammond and Youngs (2002), among many others, clearly show that, again, NCLB's mandates are agenda-driven, not legitimately research based. Slavin (2003) sheds a great deal of light on the staggering array of research manipulations common when research is molded to fit an agenda instead of examining data to draw warranted conclusions, noting cherry picking, bottom fishing, and pre-post studies as misleading uses of data, Slavin identifies many of the modes of research abuse behind NCLB mandates. The great irony is that while touting high scientific standards, NCLB and its creators repeatedly implement the worst science and data analysis possible. In teacher preparation, the Bush administration is actively attempting to remove state control of teacher training and proclaiming the entire field of education irrelevant. Scientific research is the tool this administration is wielding to dismantle teaching as any sort of profession, the advantage of such being a cheap labor force in a privatized school system.

• • •

"Policy makers, those who govern public education and appropriate the funds to pay for it, have made clear they believe teachers and administrators cannot be trusted to advance the education of all children," states Mizell (2003) in his call for teachers to claim professionalism for the education field. Long before NCLB, the power of standardized high-stakes tests loomed over students and teachers. Mizell's point is accurate—the high value placed on standardized tests reflects the lack of trust in teachers by the American public, whose taxes fund public education.

High-stakes tests (SAT scores determining scholarships, end-of-course exams determining course credit, exit exams determining graduation) have been proliferating since the early 1980s at the state level. With NCLB, states are being forced to standardize the movement with standards and tests that conform to the mandates of NCLB, or money will be lost. In this bonanza, numbers are everywhere, and it is often difficult to see the faces of any children behind all the charts and statistics.

Growing evidence suggests that while high-stakes test scores might improve, student learning often suffers; data on TAAS in Texas confirms that trend. Further, the use of standardized tests based on clearly prescribed standards creates a dynamic that negatively impacts the usefulness of the data drawn from the exams. The work and commentary of Kohn (2000), Popham (2001a), Amrein and Berliner (2002), and Lewis (2002) reveal disturbing issues at the core of the high-stakes testing movement and the proclivity to teach to the tests:

• High-stakes tests tend to reduce the curriculum to covering only what is assessed. Hillocks (2003) has shown such a phenomenon clearly in writing instruction dictated by state assessment in five representative states, with inauthentic and negative results on students' writing ability.

• Teaching to the test has moral implications, and the practice corrupts the credibility of the data drawn from the tests. When teachers teach to the tests, in other words, the numbers we gather are rendered corrupt and the entire process, futile.

• Standardization of curriculum, instruction, and assessment may not be a desirable goal for education in a free democracy.

- High-stakes tests in selected-response form are driven more by manageability and cost-effectiveness than by best practice in assessment (supported by decades of research).

- Standardized tests have a long history of issues concerning fairness in race, sex, and socioeconomic status; schools that most need federal funding will often lose that funding because of their low test scores, scores that are highly correlated with the given socioeconomic status of the students who take the exam. In SC, the state report card scores are highly correlated with the poverty indexes of the schools; most of the school report card scores are directly correlated with the poverty indexes of the schools, and schools are in effect being punished for the coincidental student population that they serve.

• • •

So far NCLB appears to be of concern only to state departments of education, colleges of education, and K–12 schools; yet, the legislation has potentially far-reaching impacts on the entire academic world. This set of mandates takes key issues and controversies out of the academic realm and puts them into the purview of the federal government—not even, notably, in the context of the free market that so many on the right espouse. These issues include the tension between quantitative and qualitative research, the value of colleges of education, and what constitutes valid research.

NCLB's first assault on academia is its brazen pronouncement on what counts as research, on what numbers matter. The Bush administration has essentially turned back the academic clock to a time when only experimental and quasi-experimental studies garnered any value (Yatvin, 2002). The past 40 years have seen a boiling and vital debate grow about the value of qualitative research and about the actual objectivity of traditional experimental research (see Lagemann, 2000, for a discussion of this evolution specifically related to educational research). The debate within the academic world over what counts as research is central to the survival of education in a free society; once the federal government has the power to dictate and thus override academic assertions, democracy is in jeopardy. Researchers all along the spectrum of methodologies must be free of governmental mandates to wrestle with their field; such open academic debate is essential to a living democracy of free people.

As well, for decades many colleges and universities have struggled over whether education was valid as a professional field. That debate certainly has value, and people lining up on either side need to be heard. But, again, this is a debate that should be left to higher education, a debate that should be left to those people in the field—not handed over to the federal government or argued from an ideological position by those with disproportionate power to prescribe. While colleges and universities have for many decades had healthy debates about what counts as credible content (Is educational pedagogy a field?, for example), that must remain a free and open debate, as with the status of research, not impinged upon by federal mandates.

Finally, several issues discussed so far have shown that when government itself gets into the business of scientific research, the process recognized as legitimate by the academic world is at the very least corrupted. It is not far-fetched to see NCLB's mandates on research and its own careless use and analysis of data as threats to the valuable academic contributions made by scholars of postmodernism, feminism, race, and gay/lesbian issues.

The mandates of NCLB are, in reality, an attack on American schools and on academia in a free nation. It is the responsibility of all in education to reject this ideological assault and reclaim those arenas of debate that belong within the academic community.

Numbers as Smoke and Mirrors—NCLB as Flawed Mandate

In some ways, NCLB is nothing new as a political answer to an educational problem. Though as I have discussed above, it does set some precedents as a federal assault on education directly and as a prescription for reframing our society indirectly. If NCLB is to be dismantled, as it should be, we have to look closely at the numerous flaws in the mandates.

One emerging weakness of NCLB is the growing concern over the face on Bush's educational policy, Rod Paige, father of the Texas Miracle and Education Secretary. As many have suspected, the Texas Miracle that led to Paige's appointment and served as a model for NCLB may be more smoke than fire. On the surface, Paige and his miracle had everything the Bush administration desired in attacking education and raising Bush's own political capital—a state with high standards and a track record for high-stakes testing, a student population high in children of color and children in poverty, and a person who had risen to be a leader in educational accountability. But things have begun to sour.

Schemo and Fessenden (2003) introduce their readers to Rosa Arevelo, a face not a number. It appears that growing evidence suggests that Rosa's experience is a better reflection of Texas education than the myth of the Miracle. Rosa's story includes:

> At the University of Houston . . . Ms. Arevelo discovered the distance between what Texas public schools called success and what she needed to know. Trained to write five-paragraph "persuasive essays" for the state exam, she was stumped by her first writing assignment [in college]. She failed the college entrance exam in math twice, even with a year of remedial algebra. At 19, she gave up and went to trade school.

This is not an isolated example. Cavanaugh (2003) reports that it is typical for state assessments to be poor indicators of college success. Further, the many touted accomplishments by Paige in Texas are proving to be distortions at best and false at worst. When TAAS results are compared with national tests, the numbers fail Paige's claims, although Dr. Paige himself offers an odd explanation that actually suggests the failure of high-stakes testing and raising standards: "TAAS and Stanford tests could not be compared because the Texas test gauges mastery of the Texas curriculum while the Stanford test measures a more general notion of what children should know in a given grade" (Schemo & Fessenden, 2003). In other words, Texas teachers, like most across the nation, are merely teaching to the test, not to what matters. Heaping irony on irony, Dr. Paige also blames "statistical anomalies" for the discrepancies concerning Texas student achievement (Schemo & Fessenden, 2003). Live by the numbers, die by the numbers?

The Texas Miracle does serve as a model for educators concerned with improving education, but not the sort of model Bush and Paige intended. Rosa Arevelo is the face of what happens to students when schooling becomes about fulfilling prescriptions; she was trained to write *to comply with the false templates of Texas's state testing*, but she could not *compose* at any level of competence that is meaningful to her as a scholar, as a young woman. Texas and Dr. Paige actually disprove through a body of evidence, through a growing swell of numbers, the efficacy of dictating standards and driving all education by high-stakes test results.

The problems do not end there. Similar to the work of the NRP and to the internal research conducted for Open Court, the success in Texas is being questioned for its own numbers games, "Education 'Miracle' Has a Math Problem," reads one headline. "'It is all phony; it's like Enron'"—this quote included in the article offers us a few troubling points (Dobbs, 2003). It seems that much of the Texas Miracle grows from distorted data and that when we do apply "business-style accountability" we inherit business-style scandal (Dobbs, 2003). When schooling is reduced to numbers—test scores, drop-out rates, profit margins—we have a mess, not a miracle. The numbers and faces are beginning to show more clearly that the paradigm NCLB is based upon is nothing more than smoke and mirrors; in other words, politics.

Piling on top of the growing realization that NCLB has sprung from questionable stock is the weight of complying with the mandates themselves:

> State officials are so overwhelmed by the data they must collect under federal education reform that many are releasing "school report cards" riddled with errors or delayed for so long that the information is virtually useless to parents and schools. (Banchero, 2003)

Much of the stated reason for NCLB's mandates revolve around accountability; that means in many states the issuing of report cards on school quality. That process is designed to encourage schools to try harder, but it also is supposed to give parents evidence for school choice. Two problems there. In my home state of SC, PACT data may be used to retain students, but the data has yet to be available before October of the following year, over 2 months *after* the students have begun the next school year. As well, in states offering school choice, parents are not getting any data on schools until well into the next school year; are they supposed to move mid-year?

Banchero (2003) includes in her article a troubling list of problems inherent with gathering so much data and disaggregating so much data. Beyond the problems with gathering and displaying the numbers behind NCLB, other complaints are being raised. Banchero and Little (2003) have revealed that in Illinois, 34,261 mistakes within the testing and data gathering bonanza have affected 75% of schools and incorrectly listed 368 schools as failing NCLB guidelines. Many successful alternative schools fear the mandates; "the state testing program poses a unique challenge: how to maintain the integrity of their vision while complying with state law" (Pardington, 2003). And special education has proven to be a virtual nightmare for both schools and the federal officials attempting to manage NCLB mandates and the unique situations involved concerning students with special needs (Silverman, 2003). As I will discuss later, NCLB shows just how senseless educational reform can be when it comes from political officials who speak and practice simplistic approaches to change and to education:

> Perhaps a future federal commission, one which starts with youth as well as with schools, will take the wisdom of these two forays into a search for fresh policies that reflect the hard facts of what it is to be an adolescent in 21st-century America—inside *and* outside of "school." (Sizer, 2003)

• • •

The federal aspect of this problem is not the only issue though. Yes, we need to move educational reform into the hands of educators, and we need to shift our concerns to the students, not the tests, not the numbers. Apparently, leaving the standards movement in the hands of states, however, offers no better solution (Darling-Hammond, 2003), especially when the states scramble to comply with NCLB. Hammond (2003) reports that state standards vary: "The study found huge differences in how much states expect their students to learn." This study from Portland, Oregon, suggests something like the dilemma that Dr. Paige raised about comparing TAAS scores with national tests; somehow standards don't match from state to state:

> Colorado set its reading proficiency standards so low that 82 percent of fifth-graders nationwide meet them, the study says. South Carolina defined fifth-grade reading proficiency so high, only 27 percent of the nation's fifth-graders read that well. (Hammond, 2003)

It appears that NCLB has created a climate for school choice after all. If students in SC wish to be better students, they should just move to Colorado, and, Boom!, their scores will rise. Like the Texas Miracle, the concept of standards itself is proving to be simply a smoke screen, unattainable and undesirable.

• • •

The weight of its own numbers is beginning to stress NCLB. This most recent attempt at prescribing the education of America's children in our public schools has internal problems that seem to suggest why these external cracks have appeared. "No Child Left Behind creates an artificial environment that bears little resemblance to the real world of schools, much less to responsible policy making," Harvey (2003) argues (p. 18). This policy is destined to collapse under its own weight, much like the former USSR. Harvey explains that NCLB sets its own standards bar too high, calling for 100% achievement, and fails in its funding, especially in terms of funding what it requires states to implement. Further, Harvey notes that NCLB tramples on a long-standing belief in local control for education; again, I add, this is ironic as it comes from a political party that has been associated with local control for many decades.

The greatest weakness, I believe, that Harvey (2003) identifies in NCLB is its complete disregard for "best practice with respect to evaluation" (p. 20). The federal government's own sense of numbers, measurement, and statistical and scientific practices makes this legislation feeble in its promise for education, but deadly in its ultimate impact on public schools:

> Testing experts have long agreed that interpreting standardized tests in isolation is not a credible summary of what individual students know or are able to do . . . . Experts also argue that using single scores for important education decisions—such as whether to promote a student, grant a diploma, or fund a school—is akin to education malpractice. (Harvey, 2003, p. 20)

Harvey recognizes that NCLB is politics, not good policy.

Elmore (2003), in another condemnation of Bush's initiative, sees NCLB as terribly flawed in its central component, accountability, interestingly, where the numbers are. He believes the law places too much emphasis on the testing, on the results and not the processes leading to assessment of learning or leading to measuring the quality of a school. Further, Elmore notes that NCLB mandates misapply current understanding of change and improvement, offer strange incentives in the form of funding that actually lowers accountability in some states, and attempt to dictate from afar (disregarding local control advantages, a point supported by Harvey [2003]).

It's Not So Simple—Addressing Literacy and Poverty

At the nexus of all these concerns is that the federal government and one particular cultural ideology through NCLB, the weight of federal legislation, are directly impacting literacy education of free people.

Literacy education is the most important and most fragile aspect of public schooling. Reading and writing are central to individual empowerment and to the security of a free people. Let's look here at how we might address literacy education to insure such individual empowerment, to protect the U.S. democracy, as a contrast to the issues discussed earlier with NCLB. We have a need to save the language from the onslaught of numbers.

I recently sat filtering through an e-mail service, one of many I receive, that highlights education-related pieces in the papers throughout America. A comment in one article has been spinning through my mind ever since. I can't find the article or remember the comment verbatim now so I'll paraphrase, feeling secure that this is fair since the sentiment is repeated endlessly these days; this was no isolated comment or belief. In response to state standards and state testing, and to NCLB, a local administrator stated flatly in the paper that the school's job with the impoverished students who were doing poorly on the language arts tests was simple; all the schools needed to do was to break down the standards into manageable pieces and teach them to those children. Ta-da!

From politicians, administrators, teachers, and the public, a chorus of "It's simple, just simplify!" seems to be blossoming in the face of high-stakes tests and federal mandates, especially when faced with reading and writing instruction for low-performing (and often impoverished) students. Therein lies the problem; our impoverished students are being cheated by the growing reductionistic mind-set in our schools as much if not more than by their socioeconomic disadvantages. Further, teaching to the test has many potential flaws, but its direct influence on instructional strategies and its supplanting of sound learning theories are beginning to harm greatly the students who need our education system the most, our impoverished students and our children born into languages other than English. Numbers are mounting to insure that these children fail, despite comments to the contrary (as we will also explore with school choice).

Well-Intentioned Misconceptions

NCLB has placed in the popular psyche now the concept of basing education decisions on scientific evidence. Despite the many flaws that dozens of educators and researchers are showing with NCLB's mandates concerning research and scientific evidence (Lemann, 2001; Yatvin, 2002; Krashen, 2002a; Darling-Hammond & Youngs, 2002), let's look closely at the central phenomenon I believe is at the heart of harmful instructional strategies that have sprung directly from research, harmful instruction that is greatly pronounced for impoverished, low-performing students.

I call this phenomenon the *not-"if"-but-"how" dilemma*. For reading and writing instruction, phonemic awareness and grammatical awareness are the areas where the phenomenon is most pronounced. A great deal of research on reading and writing over the past century clearly shows that good readers (fluent readers with high comprehension) have high phonemic awareness and that effective writers (fluent writers who express themselves well and with variety and voice) have high grammatical dexterity, including a command of Standard English and the ability to manipulate it.

From that body of research, a century of debate has simmered—often reducing the argument to *if* teachers should teach phonics and grammar, instead of *how* phonemic awareness (and more importantly, comprehension and fluency) and grammatical dexterity (and more importantly, written expression in authentic pieces) can be fostered. When we look closely at underperforming students in reading and writing, when we look closely at the classes those students are funneled into, when we look closely at the instructional strategies implemented by the teachers for those students, four misconceptions are common and are now being dramatized both by NCLB and misguided (and numbers-driven) reactions to the law:

- Since phonemic awareness and grammatical dexterity appear to be key qualities in able readers and writers, we often place our emphasis on those characteristics at the expense of the primary goal of language arts instruction: mature and independent readers and writers. For many decades, we have—again, quite often with the low-achieving students from poverty and languages other than English—allowed isolated, selected-response tests on phonics and grammar to represent reading and writing, while never having students actually perform either. We are often apt to put too much effort into training students in phonemic awareness and grammatical competency *in isolation*, while ignoring the need to engage students in authentic reading and writing.

• When students perform poorly on reading and writing (holistic performances), our default solution to addressing these weaknesses is to isolate those skills and to teach them directly and out of context. Without regard to brain research, learning styles, or multiple intelligences, we *assume* that weak students are analytical learners who need everything broken into little pieces so they can build understanding from part to whole. Wrong. Humans are significantly diverse in their learning styles and abilities, even low-performing students from impoverished backgrounds. To make a blanket assumption that all low-performing students need isolated and direct instruction is to misunderstand completely literacy development.

• A closely related assumption is that all low-performing students are linear thinkers; we believe that eclectic or chaotic experiences are automatically beyond students who show below-grade abilities in reading and writing. Not only do we isolate and decontextualize reading and writing skills, but also we struggle to organize the isolated instruction as if those isolated skills of reading and writing have some sort of inherent and prescribed order in which to be learned. Just as we cannot assume that all impoverished students are analytical thinkers, we cannot assume they all need linear instruction as well. Further, that literacy ability can be fragmented and then placed into a clear sequence to be learned is simply a false hope, though it makes for easier implementation of instruction and testing.

• Once students have shown weaknesses in their reading and writing, they are most often subjected to much more highly structured and prescriptive classes, instruction, and assignments. Large amounts of worksheets and repetitive practice with isolated skills still dominate remedial classes disproportionately filled with our lowest socioeconomic students. A long-entrenched practice with weaker students is to give them templates and prescriptions for reading and writing (recall Rosa Arevelo from Texas). From their first to their last years in school, they read textbook passages and answer closed-ended questions that move from knowledge to evaluation on Bloom's taxonomy, and they write template essays with stilted introductions (and the obligatory thesis that details three points), bodies, and conclusions. We never allow them to experiment with authentic engaged reading and writing because we demand that they show us surface mastery first and perform fill-in-the-blank activities, as if the surface mastery and template performance matter more than the authentic acts.

These four misconceptions combine to create course work that is more and more abstracted from the reality of authentic reading and writing, isolating low-performing students more and more from the real goals of literacy instruction. Ironically, decades of research have shown best practice for integrated reading and writing instruction (Zemelman, Daniels & Hyde, 1998), but the lowest performing students are least likely to be in classes where best practice is implemented, while the more successful students (often students of relative affluence) are in honors or advanced classes engaged in authentic and integrated reading and writing opportunities.

Making the Connection

Ultimately, when addressing the reading and writing needs of our student population impoverished both socioeconomically and linguistically, the job is *not* simple, it is not even to *simplify*, but it is something we can do—if we take the right steps (Allington, 2002; Moore & O'Neill, 2002; Weaver, 1996; Wilhelm, Baker, & Dube, 2001; Routman, 1996; Routman, 2003). Best practice in reading and writing instruction must be holistic, integrated, and authentic for all students; five guiding principles can serve as starting points for the change, and they can serve students, teachers, and schools well even under the weight of NCLB and high-stakes measurements of learning:

Start all reading and writing instruction with authentic student performances of reading and writing. To impose or to foster?—that is the question. For too long, we have approached the acts of reading and writing as if they are fluids we can simply pour into the empty vessels, our students. When our students are impoverished, we are even more likely to see nearly empty vessels. Although reading and writing are artificial verbal acts, when compared to speaking and listening, they are performances that spring from humans' natural verbal capacity prewired, as it were, in the brain. We must begin to have students perform as readers and writers to give the teachers direct evidence upon which to base instruction. Those performances must be by choice: Students select what they want to read and offer what they are inspired to respond, and students choose both the topic and form of their writing. From those performances, a teacher can then begin to foster the demonstrated strengths of those students and to address directly the revealed weaknesses and misconceptions in the students' works. Additionally, impoverished students often perform poorly on language arts assessment because they have had impoverished backgrounds in literacy in their homes; real, engaged reading and writing will help bridge that gap, not prescribed and organized worksheets that serve mainly to collect numbers on those students and to document their failures.

Insure student awareness of the social realities and social expectations of reading and writing outside of formal schooling. Advocates of holistic and integrated approaches to fostering literacy development are often inappropriately labeled as somehow being against the teaching of phonics and grammar. Again the *not-"if"-but-"how"* dilemma. There should be no argument about *if* students need phonemic awareness or a command of Standard English; the debate centers on *how* to foster those abilities. Teachers dealing with literacy have to juggle continuously the authentic performances of the students (the shifting evidence of where each student is as a reader and writer) *and* the relationship between those performances and the social realities and expectations of literacy. Students must be made aware of the broad spectrum of ways to respond to and use reading, along with the cultural capital that those reactions carry. Students must be made aware of the values that are attached in our society to a person's conforming to Standard English. Especially for the impoverished and low-performing student, the *how* in addressing those social issues becomes both powerfully important and complicated. Nonetheless, we must begin with where each student is; then foster with each student where society expects her to be, eventually empowering that student to move purposefully and fluidly within the realm of reading and writing as she desires, both personally and as an engaged member of society.

Increase student reading and writing of nonfiction. I mean no sarcasm here, but Keats's claim about beauty and truth may be lost on many of our students, especially those who are faced daily with issues of survival. The need for art, the need for poetry, fiction, and drama is a supreme one. As a poet myself and a visual art and music lover, I am eager to introduce all my students to the world of beauty and truth. But, I am also firmly convinced that we shortchange all students in our tendency to emphasize the so-called creative genres to the exclusion of nonfiction. From a practical perspective, students are far more likely to need to read and write nonfiction in their daily lives than to interact with poetry, fiction, and drama. As well, I have found that low-performing students in language arts classes are more quickly engaged in nonfiction writing, nonfiction movies, and nonfiction composition, especially with personal narratives and persuasive works. Yet, we must be careful not to assume nonfiction to be less difficult, it isn't, or less creative, it isn't. Every reading strategy, every writing technique can be addressed with nonfiction as with fiction, poetry, and drama. Nonfiction simply adds for many students the aspects of practicality and engagement.

Integrate reading and writing instruction authentically. One of the most challenging dilemmas for literacy instruction is integrating reading and writing authentically. I have never found a simple solution, but I have had success with constant reflection as a teacher. When I engage my students in reading and writing, I simply question myself about the assignments: What do they accomplish? Am I asking students to perform in a way that promotes learning, or does it merely fulfill some academic requirement? Ultimately, "authentic" activities must include a few key elements—student choice, appropriate time to perform, and expert feedback from the teacher (Atwell, 1998). The impoverished and struggling students need those authentic experiences dramatically since they often have fewer such experiences in their daily lives when compared to their more affluent peers. Notably, these characteristics are necessarily *absent* from high-stakes testing and most of the components of accountability found in NCLB, mainly since they offer insurmountable problems with reducing these aspects to numbers on a single-sitting exam.

Reconstruct the courses for low performing students and mandate a change in the experience levels of the teachers instructing those courses. One of the ugliest secrets of public education is the instructional caste system: Veteran teachers get the good kids, and new teachers have to earn those good kids by years of teaching the low achievers. Teaching reading and writing holistically to low-performing students with large gaps in their verbal skills is one of the most challenging things a teacher can do, and *only* the most experienced and well-trained teacher can do that job well; those teachers, by the way, need much more than simply content knowledge to be effective. I will make this short: Our most socioeconomically deprived students must be in classes with low student-teacher ratios and with veteran and well-trained teachers.

• • •

Another piece about education filtered past me not too long ago. It seems that some research is showing that when impoverished students are mixed with more affluent peers, the impoverished students improve in their verbal skills dramatically when compared both with isolated impoverished students and the more affluent peers. I think this news is promising, but also very complicated since so many factors go into that formula. Yet, I feel secure suggesting all that I have argued above. Our low-achieving and impoverished students need the reading/writing connection because it is their best connection to the rest of their lives. Numbers, federal mandates, and the like will not serve us well in the education that matters most—literacy.

Discrediting Schools by the Numbers— Why Vouchers and Choice Fail

While NCLB speaks often of science and research, as I suggested in Chapter One, no one in the U.S. goes very far before the lure of money raises its head. Yes, capitalism is a strong paradigm in the American psyche and how we see numbers, and it is also a driving force behind federal legislation concerning our schools. From Reagan to Bush, federal mandates placed on our schools have indirectly and directly foisted onto America a call for privatizing schools, though support for school choice and vouchers remains lukewarm among most of us. In the last 5 or 10 years, at both the federal and state levels, this call for replacing public education with a free market model has grown among politicians, who have begun to cloak that call in a concern for the poor, for those left behind by our public schools. Numbers are flying daily comparing schools in every imaginable pairing—state to state, district to district, public to private, etc.; yet those numbers and large sums of money studying school choice appear to be solving almost nothing ("No Victory," 2003). What, then, should we believe about choosing between choice or public schools?

• • •

The small-town high school football team has been in decline for nearly 20 years after several decades of success, highlighted by a number of state championships. Despite the decades of failure, the town still cares, and the people come each Friday night in the fall to watch. Why? Because a public school is far more than teaching and learning, far more than a political football, far more than the numbers on a school report card, far more than Average Yearly Progress (AYP, an NCLB measure of school worth).

Supreme Court decisions and political rhetoric have escalated recent attacks on public education. Against such an assault as discussed above, Americans in general and educators in particular need to defend one of the most crucial aspects of our democracy, public schools. Not just public education—that is merely one part of a much bigger, much more important element of our society, our free society, our democracy.

As an educator, a parent, and an American, one who cherishes our commitment to life, liberty, and the pursuit of happiness, I am calling for a renewed defense of public schools, and a wholehearted rejection of vouchers in particular, and arguments for school choice in the larger scheme. The numbers just simply do not support that public education fails us, and they certainly do not support that a competition model will save our children.

Yes, public schools are failing in some areas, and far too many students are not being served effectively by the current system. But community-based schools open to all is the system we must defend and improve for the sake of our democracy. Ultimately, vouchers and choice are not the solutions to our educational deficiencies, but much can be done by educators to raise the effectiveness of our current public school system, a system that is essential to America remaining "the land of the free."

• • •

Let's begin with the essential flaws in the arguments for vouchers and choice; then we can see why public schools are crucial to America and its children.

First, many choice proponents have fallen victim to a silver-bullet mentality. The voucher and choice arguments suffer from an essential logic problem with any proposed solutions to complex problems. Vouchers and choice are touted (like a number of other proposals—lowering class size, raising teacher pay, equipping schools with

more and better computers, etc.) as a silver bullet for improvement.
The truth is that *no single action* can help with a complex set of problems, especially in idiosyncratic endeavors like teaching and learning.
Those aspects that negatively impact education and varied schools in
Nebraska, South Carolina, and New York are of such vast differences
that single-solution thinking becomes laughable; federal templates for
improvement will certainly fail more schools than they could help.
Vouchers and choice in and of themselves cannot magically improve
education, though advocates speak as if they can.

Second, vouchers and choice as solutions for American schools
are political ones, not educational ones. The greatest impetus behind
vouchers and choice come from politicians and social pundits; in rare
cases the support also comes from educrats, more concerned with
administration than teaching and learning. A telling fact about the
movement is that practitioners and educational researchers are far
less likely to support vouchers and choice and more apt to reveal the
abundant flaws with the proposals. Politicians are drawn to simplistic
solutions, and as Bracey (1997a) has shown, politicians and educrats
have long attempted to gain political capital by trashing existing education and promising great improvements. The vouchers and choice
movement is yet another point in that continuum, and like other political solutions before it, the vouchers movement has little to do with
improving teaching and learning; it has far more to do with a social
commitment to the capitalistic ideal, to a nearly fanatical marriage
with free market ideology. As I discussed above, it's not as simple as
numbers make it appear.

A third significant, but ignored, issue in the choice debate is existing school buildings. Communities across America have invested
millions of dollars in physical *schools*. Vouchers and choice would
create senseless problems with those school buildings across America.
Even if a voucher system is limited to public schools, consider this
potential situation: A school district has seven public high schools;
high school D has the highest assessment scores in the state on the
school report cards one year so all the parents want their children to
attend that school, a school building that holds only 750 students, the
next year. (We're pretending all the data is correctly provided to parents in time for such a decision.) The state moves in portables and six
schools are abandoned. At the end of that year, as is the nature of
testing when populations increase so dramatically, scores drop! This
may seem exaggerated, but the constant fluctuation of school choices

based on single-year scores would be a needless and counter-educational disaster; the voucher and choice movement is simply ignoring the tremendous (and avoidable) physical plant problem that would be created for an experiment that has little to do with improving teaching and learning. Existing school buildings are often the center of communities, and America must choose to keep that system and those investments intact. Each school is far more than its rating on the school report card or how well it complies with NCLB.

At the heart of this debate as well is another tension we have been flirting with all along, capitalism v. democracy. Engel (2000) poses an argument that voucher and choice movements are wedded to capitalistic ideology *at the expense of democracy*. I cannot improve on his argument, though I do accept his premise. The public school that draws its students from the community where it sits is crucial for the survival of democracy because this system of schools is a microcosm of our country. Communities are both cultural institutions and evolving melting pots simultaneously. The schools in each community serve to reinforce the American ideal of democracy.

Further, voucher and choice proponents argue that public schools are a monopoly; this argument is a false analogy. Capitalism as an economic system rightfully rejects monopolies, but a true monopoly, one that is a threat to American ideals, is a person or group of people who command sole power over a service or product for *inflated financial gain*. This last component—inflated financial gain—is not a part of the public school system. Like police forces or the military or the judicial system, public schools are a social service that is necessary for the survival of our democracy and our capitalistic system of economics; public schools are not profit making entities, and they should never become such. If we falsely impose profit-making onto schools to force them to conform to market ideology, we are more likely to bring the downside of the business world (corruption and greed) than to improve the education of children.

Public schools are microcosms of the community where students live *and* the fountainhead of the ideal American community. Dewey (1938) and a host of progressive educators have argued for a century that the community and democratic values of public education are as, if not more, important as academic learning. Public schools not distorted by parental choice fostered within a free market paradigm, which could segregate schools by a great host of criteria, help insure that American children will learn to function within the smaller community of a school before stepping into the greater community of their towns and their states and their country. Community schools help create all that makes up "community," pride grown from who we are and what we do.

We must also ask how competition will force schools to improve during a teacher shortage. While some who champion vouchers and choice believe no teacher shortage exists (and it appears that NCLB might insure that anyone can be licensed, thus creating a conveniently large and cheap work force), most today accept that a shortage of qualified teachers is a problem. If the qualified teacher pool is low, from where will the new teachers come when new schools are formed? Vouchers will only create a shuffling of teachers; it will not insure that teacher quality increases; it will not raise the bar for incoming teachers. The realistic actuality is that new schools will choose weaker applicants to save money (many private schools already do so) and that a senseless teacher shuffling will occur much like the jumping from school building to school building could occur. Just as the moving from school to school causes no improvement for students, stirring and probably diluting our teacher pool would not benefit students either.

Fullan (1991) has shown that the change process requires 10 years to evaluate the effectiveness of change initiatives. The voucher and choice movements both disregard this research and work against any hope of evaluating vouchers and choice themselves; a free-for-all choice frenzy could shuffle student and teacher populations each year as testing data is released. The voucher movement hopes that the threat of clients (both parents and students are seen as clients by voucher proponents; oddly, students are seen as products as well in this contorted business paradigm) leaving a service will force a service to perform better. If that threat can work at all—and I doubt that schools are underperforming merely because they feel unthreatened—it will create a climate that rewards quick and superficial *appearances* of success, not lasting and real change for improvement; such an occurrence has already raised its ugly head in the growing rush to teach to high-stakes tests, an unethical and misleading phenomenon (Popham, 2001b; Dobbs, 2003; Schemo & Fessenden, 2003). The current public school system is the only format that maintains enough consistency of populations to evaluate the big picture of educational progress. A constantly shifting population of students would make true assessment of educational success even more cumbersome.

The overwhelming data on who chooses when choice and vouchers are made available is a telling sign; those who take advantage of choice are the most wealthy and most well-educated within any population given options (Engel, 2000). The irony, of course, is that the least wealthy and least well-educated are the most atrisk for failing in school settings; thus, it is clear that vouchers and choice do not address those most atrisk within the public educational system. While there will always be tension in a free society over how much that society can or should interfere in the lives of individuals, it seems that public education *as a social institution designed to insure the welfare of a democracy* has a moral obligation to provide the guidance and education that children might miss from the lack of guidance found in the home. Yes, this is a touchy subject, teetering on an intrusive government taking inappropriate matters into its own hands. But in the end, we must teeter. Holton (2003), in his response to *A Nation at Risk*, made a similar argument about "the danger to a cohesive, healthy American society if the public school system is undermined," and he notes that even Thomas Jefferson saw a need for the federal government to directly protect public education, not dismantle it as many recent administrations seem to be determined to do.

An often ignored problem with vouchers and choice is the hidden expense of being mobile enough to attend schools not in ones community; simply put, choice requires not only that parents be capable consumers, but that parents be financially able and free to transport children to any school they may choose. Again, those students most in need of better schools, the impoverished, are most likely not to have access to transportation to attend schools many miles away (Medina, 2003). Voucher programs have yet to address the large hidden cost of having choice restricted by a child's access to transportation. Further, many areas of the country have few people per square mile; other schools are not accessible because of sheer distance even if the families have transportation. As with physical school buildings and the availability of qualified teachers, transportation is a third aspect of the voucher and choice movement that makes such impractical.

Let's also ask: Will private school vouchers insure 100% coverage? Many voucher programs are little more than subsidies to middle- and upper-class families who choose private schools that have costs far above the amount of the voucher. Vouchers as mere subsidies, part of the cost of attending a school, again is not addressing the population of students at greatest risk for failure, the students most likely to be left behind. Many politicians tout $2,500 vouchers for families who have a choice of private schools that cost $6,000. How does this provide choice for the poor? Combined with the hidden expenses of choice, real costs of choice will invariably alienate those most in need of better schools.

To counter this cry from politicians, we must consider existing and ongoing educational research, being certain to separate objective studies from research and data interpretations with hidden agendas. Many writing about education (Bracey, 1997a; Engel, 2000, for examples) have pointed to numerous worldwide experiments in choice and voucher systems; the research has shown that often both the chosen schools and the abandoned schools are affected negatively by the choice process. There is no compelling educational research that shows that vouchers or school choice will actually spur any changes in education that will benefit student learning and achievement. Belief in the voucher movement is little more than idealism extrapolated from a somewhat blind allegiance to capitalistic paradigms of free-market ideology. Of course the free-market paradigm is a valuable one in issues of commerce, but it fails as a universal paradigm, especially in the core social institutions of a democratic society.

The voucher and choice movement will only add fuel to a ridiculous fire over the separation of church and state. First let's look at the issue of separation of church and state in the context of its cousin, the right to bear arms. Both issues have evolved into fundamental beliefs within our democracy, beliefs that are tenuous at best in their inception. If taken literally and in the context of its creation, the Second Amendment provides the right to bear arms *for the forming of a militia,* not just because anyone wants to own a gun. But Americans have come to accept the spirit of the amendment, ignoring the militia stipulation. Such is the case with the separation of church and state; it matters little if and when and how the concept came into the American psyche; most Americans rightfully fear the negative impacts religion can have on the state and the state can have on religion. Vouchers and choice often create problems of separation where they did not exist before. With vouchers and choice, we would needlessly erode a barrier that is essential to the survival of America.

With these issues, we can start to see that in its essence choice is a failed and primarily politically motivated manipulation of our schools. If improving our democracy through the educating of our children is our goal, then choice is a false start at best and a dead end for our nation at worst.

• • •

How is this movement for school choice relevant in this discussion of numbers, science, and federal mandates concerning education? Gehring (2003) and Ralph G. Neas (2003), president of People for the American Way, have noted that the federal government through NCLB now "is providing millions of dollars in grants to a handful of pro-voucher and privatization groups." The numbers don't lie here. The federal dollars being funneled to organizations that stand to profit if schools are handed over to the private realm should make us pause, and revolt.

Let's, then, reject the cry for vouchers and choice—a cry that is wasting valuable time and energy that would be better spent on the welfare of children—and turn our energies to choosing public schools. But this recommitment to public schools should entail a re-creating of those schools. There is no need to remain committed to all the flaws in the current system, but there is a moral imperative to choose public schooling as the central component of a democracy. That commitment should include the following re-creations:

Address low student-teacher ratios at the K4 through fifth grade levels. While the efficacy of reducing student/teacher ratios is clearly debatable, Biddle and Berliner (2002) offer a solid body of research that does support the need to monitor closely the ratio at K4 through fifth grades. The earliest years of schooling are the most important in the life of a child, especially in terms of literacy development. Throughout America, high school students commonly sit in advanced classes of 10 or so students while in the same district, primary and elementary students are packed into classes of 30–35 with that teacher alone in the room. This numerical inequity is common and must be changed. Along with that reduction at the early grades, though, we must demand that teacher practices change as well. Student-teacher ratios in and of themselves are no more a silver bullet than choice, if we are honest here.

Overhaul teacher education programs—particularly concerning coursework and approaches to teacher planning. Teacher education and the recertifying and retraining of in-service teachers must be completely reexamined, though not as Bush and Paige would suggest, not to create a cheap workforce but to create highly qualified teachers. The balance of content work with direct training in education courses is greatly skewed. Again, primary and elementary teachers are often the most improperly prepared in teacher education programs. They are sadly undereducated about language acquisition and about the huge range of content they are supposed to cover. And in their classrooms they are more frequently being asked to cover far too much content *for the sake of testing* while the students receive little effective instruction or experience in reading and writing, the essential skills a student must acquire to be successful in school and in life. Overall, teacher education programs, like public schools themselves, are being dictated to by accreditation and standards movements that create a blur of bureaucracy *that has little to do with authentic teaching and learning,* but a lot to do with paperwork, mindless checklists, certificates of compliance, and endless measurement.

Expand the core curriculum—reevaluating the role of elective courses. In our daily language we refer to things that do not really matter as "merely academic." Why? Part of the explanation may be that public education has wedded itself to a core curriculum for a century—a core curriculum that has reduced bodies of knowledge to mere essential hoops that must be jumped through for grades, Carnegie units, and certificates; it is the stuff of schooling, not of living. Oddly, the real world of America holds up every day for all to see that we reward most richly those who excel in fields that are just elective courses or extracurricular in school—art, band, music, physical education, drama, athletics. The fragmented curriculum and the sacred charm ascribed to certain content areas must be reconsidered if schools can become what they should be, enriching for young people to become empowered in the most free country in the world.

Make literacy central to K4 through fifth grades. In the earliest years of life, only one real area is essential, literacy development. Content knowledge is of little importance, but the ability to communicate is paramount. Because of our foolish high-stakes testing movement, we are beginning to ask the youngest of students to perform on tests that measure little more than traditionally secondary (thus, knowledge-oriented) approaches to math, English, science, and social studies. Students are bubbling frantically on easily scored tests without ever producing any ideas on their own in their own words and sentences. School has become a way to satisfy political mandates and not a place to discover oneself as a thoughtful human. Public schools must commit primary and elementary education to rich classrooms focused almost exclusively on reading and writing; the art, recess, math, science, social studies, music, and such are simply a wide variety of avenues to help each child grow in her language abilities and as a self-directed learner.

Abandon education's marriage to high-stakes testing and scope-and-sequence standards. The current mania for standards and high-stakes standardized tests is nothing new, regretfully. But this cycle does show the inherent dangers both in scope-and-sequence standards that encourage directly and indirectly the mere coverage of facts and in ascribing to standardized tests gate-keeping power. Teacher planning and instruction are dominated by teaching to the test since students' promotions and access to colleges are determined sometimes solely by standardized tests. Teaching, learning, and assessment are far more complex than dictating standards and running a score sheet through a scanner for a grade. Instead, public schools should move toward teacher authority for teaching, student-centered learning, and authentic assessment.

Call for a commitment to learning for understanding. Ultimately, the current standards movement fails because it encourages mere coverage and ignores student understanding. Howard Gardner (1991, 1999a) and works growing from his call for student understanding (Wiske, 1998; Blythe & Assoc., 1998) argue for the need to encourage student understanding of broad concepts. This paradigm shift would require moving from *content as an end for instruction* to *content as a means to understanding*.

Redesign the school day and year. Many things guide what we do in the running of public schools—tradition, tourism, athletic events, societal expectations. In many of these cases, the guiding forces have little to do with supporting or improving education. The current 8–3 school day and the yearly calendar that skips the summer months have many flaws; changes would benefit students a great deal. The traditional school day (and the traditional class period of about an hour, with students juggling as many as six to eight courses at a time) ignores a great deal of research on what best supports deep learning; the summer gap in schooling also disregards most children's need for coherence to enhance understanding. Regardless of what choices we would make for changing these functional aspects of public schools, we must balance those decisions so that student learning is *most* important—not the tourism industry, not after-school sports, not because we've always done it that way—without ignoring the many facets of schooling that also matter.

Bring a balance to the role of "teacher"—from K4 through college instruction. From public school teachers to college professors, a wide spectrum of performances and expectations exist for teachers. Along that continuum are many points that add up to the ideal educator. In reality, though, too many imbalances exist between the public school teacher and the college professor. Taking from each, I suggest that teachers at all levels should share these characteristics:

• A thorough training and commitment to the art of teaching because content expertise is not enough to be a teacher.

• A thorough training and commitment to an area or areas of content because teaching pedagogy is not enough to be a teacher.

• A commitment to a field of study *as a scholar*. Teachers at all levels should participate within the fields that they teach; English teachers should write, art teachers should create art, and the like.

• A teaching assignment that allows and requires both time to teach and time to be a scholar.

Professionalize teaching and expect teachers to be professional. Much of the last point contributes to a crucial area of need in public schooling, the professionalization of teaching. Teacher expertise (in a content field and in teaching), teacher autonomy, teacher pay, and teacher working expectations and conditions all must be restructured if public schooling is to improve significantly. The expectations and prestige afforded a kindergarten teacher is light-years away from a research physicist in a major university; there is no legitimate support for such a huge chasm. Often ignored English educator Lou LaBrant wrote in her memoirs that American schools have everything backward; we often encounter our best teachers (in terms of their preparation to teach) at the end of our learning careers, although in actuality we need them most at the beginning (Thomas, 2001). Most teachers tend to be sincere and hard working, but the system doesn't prepare or reward teachers with any equity; that inequity must stop.

Gain a voice for practicing educators in the national public debate about education. In my home state and area, the education de-

bate never seems to disappear. Oddly, the players in that debate always include the governor, other elected officials, local talk-radio per-
sonalities, and the general public, as I have shown earlier in this
discussion. Who is virtually never heard? Practicing educators. Un-
like most other professions, teaching suffers from the common conception that anyone can teach, anyone knows how schools should be
run. Such logic, though, is like saying that anyone who has ridden in
a plane is knowledgeable enough to be a pilot. One solution to this
phenomenon is that teachers themselves need to become politically
involved—in the broad sense, not the narrow one. Experts in a field
should have the dominant voice in any public debate. Lawyers
should control the debate on law; medical doctors, on medicine; engineers, on building projects; and, of course, teachers, on education. But
educators have passively allowed politicians and the person on the
street dictate what we teach and how we teach it.

• • •

No one values freedom of choice as an American ideal and a reality more than I do; that concept is much of why I have chosen education as my career. But in the essential institutions that make that
freedom of choice possible, Americans are morally bound to choosing
public institutions and rejecting privatization. As mentioned earlier
concerning the military or our police forces, for example, public
schools are the only choice for educating American children that insures the American democracy.

Choice and voucher advocates are imposing a false paradigm on
education *for the sake of the paradigm and not for the sake of teaching and
learning.* Choice is a false paradigm because choice by its nature cannot address the needs of improving education; choice as a paradigm
for improvement belongs in the business arena when the roles of consumer, products, and profit are clearly defined and pure. For schooling, those roles are either muddled or inappropriate. The problems
with educating our children in a free democracy have nothing to do
with the absence of competition; it has to do with a myriad of social
and human factors that are ever-changing and unpredictable. Education is a human endeavor; it is messy and chaotic.

Profit margins cannot be allowed to become the numbers that run
our schools. Our children deserve something of *people,* not of *numbers.*
Choosing public schools is choosing our children—and rejecting the
cult of numbers games that threaten us today.

CONCLUSION

Beyond the Numbers
to the Students We Teach

Several years ago, I had a young man in my eleventh-grade American literature class. He was fairly lazy, rarely completing his work he was assigned. One day after class, he approached me and asked if he could have a complete copy of Henry David Thoreau's "Civil Disobedience." I'll admit that my attitude about this student changed immediately.

Over the course of the year, his work was always marginal, and I believe he finished the year with a solid 70 average, exactly what he needed to pass. To many people's surprise, I asked him if he was interested in registering for my Advanced Placement Literature and Composition course, and he said he was. The principal had the student and his parents sign a release stating that they knew the AP class would be even more challenging than the course he had just barely passed. Of course, they all signed.

Why did I do this? Because I knew more about this young man than a 70 could reflect. He was and still is a nonconformist by nature; he is also extremely bright and thoughtful. Today he is completing graduate work in philosophy at a major state university. I doubt that any grades throughout his journey have shown who he is—not his SAT now long in his past, not his GPA, not his GRE. And I would bet that he has gathered a series of teachers like me who saw *him* in spite of any numbers swirling around him.

You see, numbers don't lie, but they certainly don't tell the whole story either. No numbers can capture the humanity of any student, any person. And educators such as Paulo Freire, quoted earlier, knew and know that education carries with it a frightening potential to be a tool of the oppressors. In my discussion, I have attempted to suggest that the federal government is now poised to eradicate public education as we know it in favor of capitalistic ideology. Those who believe in the competition model also believe their ideology is what is best for all. But, as Freire might argue, they are victims of their own narrow consciousness, and *to educate* is the antithesis of imposing the consciousness of those in power on the people easily oppressed by those prescriptions, neatly clothed in the language of standards.

• • •

This discussion is intended to raise our collective consciousness about schooling in America, about the urgent need to reinvent public education in a thriving democracy, about the real and present danger of numbers games in our schools. Political solutions to educational problems are feckless; only educators themselves have the knowledge and tools to make schools serve our children and our society well. I want to leave this discussion by reiterating a few changes that are crucial if we are to save and rebuild public education; this is a call we must heed now.

First, public schools must address directly and fully the types of misconceptions I have highlighted, especially in Chapter One. The forces that have pushed education in America to being primarily superficial and simplistic, an act of covering the material, are to blame for the great misconceptions many of us have concerning statistics, research, science, and even verifiable natural phenomenon. We cannot allow ideologues to manipulate our textbooks and our curriculum; we cannot have politicians, pundits, and the average person on the street dictate how teachers must teach. If it were not so important, it would be silly that in the year 2004 people are still referring to evolution as "just a theory"—that we persist to speak of it as a controversial subject *even to be identified as a real part of the scientific debate.*

Further, we must shift the focus of teaching in American schools away from behavioristic paradigms of training and toward constructivistic practices that foster learning for understanding. Behavioristic assumptions are ripe for any to turn teaching into indoctrination; this is unacceptable as even a potential problem in a free society.

Paired with our marriage with behaviorism is our weakness for quantifying. Positivism has inordinate control over how we think and act, especially in academia. That which cannot be measured, that

which cannot be reduced to numbers must gain its proper prominence in schooling. Howard Gardner calls for people to pay attention
to the Beautiful in our schools. It sounds soft to many, but we must
envision a time when that carries the sense of rigor and *value* with the
average person on the street that it deserves.

Instruction must become student centered with content being a
means, not an end, and assessment must become a tool to support
student learning and not a force to stratify our democracy to appease
the business world that needs workers, that needs a cheap labor force.
Yet, these changes cannot come about unless teachers themselves embrace their profession and claim their fields as professionals. And this
too is a question of power, of empowerment. It also is a chicken-and-
egg dilemma. Which comes first, teacher empowerment or teachers
performing as professionals to earn that empowerment? Our public
schools are places where questions of power are raised and even answered. If they increasingly become tools of the government, tools of
the elite in our society, then those questions will never be raised, or
answered.

Currently, NCLB is most successful in silencing teachers and students; that is not education, and that is not what breathes life into a
democracy. Maybe numbers don't lie after all. Maybe they carry the
weight of silencing those who need to be heard most. That is even
more frightening than a lie.

• • •

Let's return here at the end to the strange and frightening mix that
has been at the center of this discussion—the media, the pundits, the
politicians, and these things we call education and statistics. Recently,
I clicked my way through cable channels, as men are apt to do, and
paused on C-SPAN2 and its replaying of Al Franken's book tour at
the University of Missouri (the replay was November 30, 2003, of the
original talk on November 19, 2003). Franken is promoting his newest
book, *Lies and the Lying Liars Who Tell Them.*

During his talk, which was part satire and part political commentary from the Left, Franken mentioned NCLB and the political nature
of the voucher and school choice debate. Everything I have been
writing about here presented itself right there on my TV that Sunday
morning. I laughed, but much of that morning's viewing truly wasn't
funny. I am ending this book by stealing a story about statistics told
by Franken.

It seems that recent to Franken's book tour, Britt Hume had made some comments about the number of soldiers dying in Iraq in what the government had deemed a period after the war. Hume, according to Franken's reading of the comments, explained that *statistically*, average citizens were dying in California at a much more alarming rate than soldiers in Iraq; he justified the statistical truth by stating that California and Iraq are about the same geographical size. Franken paused at the comment; then he noted that the number of people in California (the population from which the death rate was drawn) is dramatically larger than the number of troops in Iraq. *That* statistical truth showed that soldiers in Iraq were about 65 times more likely to die than the average citizen in California.

Once again—varying viewpoints stating statistical truths from the same bodies of evidence. I will concede that numbers don't lie, if we can state loudly and often that people *do* die, that children *will* be left behind if we keep looking at the numbers and ignoring the people. Numbers games involve people, and educating is about human beings. "We know so very much about the trees, and miss the forest," Barbara Kingsolver (2002) notes about our American frailty—missing the big picture because of the details (pp. 141–142). *We know so very much about the numbers, and miss the children.*

REFERENCES

Abrams, L. M., & Madaus, G. F. (2003). The lessons of high-stakes testing. *Educational Leadership, 61* (3), 31–35.

Amrein, A. L., & Berliner, D. C. (2002, December). *An analysis of some unintended and negative consequences of high-stakes testing.* Tempe, AZ: Education Policy Research Unit. Available on-line: http://edpolicylab.org.

Allington, R. L. (2002, June). What I've learned about effective reading instruction from a decade of studying exemplary elementary classroom teachers. *Phi Delta Kappan, 83* (10), 740–747. Available on-line as "The Six Ts of Effective Elementary Literacy Instruction": http://www.readingrockets.org/print.php?ID=413.

Arenson, K. W. (2003, December 14). At Bard College, a plan to teach teachers more of what they're teaching. *The New York Times.*

Atwell, N. (1998). *In the middle: New understanding about writing, reading, and learning* (2nd ed.). Portsmouth, NH: Boyton/Cook.

Ayers, W. (2001). *To teach: The journey of a teacher* (2nd ed.). New York: Teachers College Press.

Baines, L. (2003, April 6). The Bozo syndrome. *Teachers College Record.* Retrieved April 8, 2003, from: http://www.tcrecord.org/PrintContent.asp?ContentID=11148.

Banchero, S. (2003, November 26). Sea of test data buries U.S. schools. *Chicago Tribune.*

Banchero, S., & Little, D. (2003, December 19). Errors fill state testing data. *Chicago Tribune.*

Baron, J., & Norman, M. F. (1992). SATs, achievement tests, and high-school class rank as predictors of college performance. *Educational and Psychological Measurements, 52* (4), 1047–1055.

Bell, B. I. (1949). *Crisis in education: A challenge to American complacency.* New York: Whittlesey House.

Benveniste, L., Carnoy, M., & Rothstein, R. (2003). *All else equal: Are public and private schools different?* New York: Routledge Falmer.

Berliner, C. B., & Biddle, B. J. (1995). *The manufactured crisis: Myths, frauds, and the attack on America's public schools.* New York: Addison-Wesley.

Bestor, A. E. (1953). *Educational wastelands: The retreat from learning in our public schools.* Urbana: University of Illinois Press.

Biddle, B. J. (1997, September). Foolishness, dangerous nonsense, and real correlates of state differences in achievement. *Phi Delta Kappan, 79* (1), 9–13.

Biddle, B. J., & Berliner, D. C. (2002). Small class size and its effects. *Educational Leadership, 59* (5), 12–23.

Blythe, T., & Associates. (1998). *The teaching for understanding guide.* San Francisco: Jossey-Bass.

Botstein, L. (1997). *Jefferson's children: Education and the promise of American culture.* New York: Doubleday.

Bracey, G. W. (2003a). April foolishness: The 20th anniversary of *A Nation at Risk. Phi Delta Kappan, 84* (8), 616–621.

———. (2003b). *On the death of childhood and the destruction of public schools: The folly of today's education policies and practices.* Portsmouth, NH: Heinemann.

———. (1997a). *Setting the record straight: Responses to misconceptions about public education in the United States.* Alexandria, VA: Association for Supervision and Curriculum Development.

———. (1997b, November). What happened to America's public schools? Not what you might think. *American Heritage, 48* (8), 38–52.

Brooks, J. G., & Brooks, M. G. (1999). *In search of understanding: The case for constructivist classrooms.* Alexandria, VA: Association for Supervision and Curriculum Development.

Brozo, W. G., & Hargis, C. (2003). Using low-stakes reading assessment. *Educational Leadership, 61* (3), 60–64.

Camara, W. J., & Echternacht, G. (2000). The SAT I and high school grades: Utility in predicting success in college. *Research Notes.* Retrieved November 5, 2003, from: http://www.collegeboard.com/research/abstract/0,3154,3869,00.html.

Camilli, G., Vargas, S., & Yurecko, M. (2003, May 8). *Teaching children to read*: The fragile link between science and federal education policy. *Education Policy Analysis Archives, 11* (15).

Cavanagh, S. (2003, October 29). Many state tests said to be poor indicators of college readiness. *Education Week, 23* (9), 13. Retrieved October 30, 2003, from: http://www.edweek.org.

Cheney, G., McMillan, J. J., & Schwartzman, R. (1997). Should we buy the "student as-consumer" metaphor? *The Montana Professor, 7* (3). Retrieved March 26, 2003, from: http://mtfrof.msun.edu/Fall1997/Cheney.html.

Childress, H. (1998, April). Seventeen reasons why football is better than high school. *Phi Delta Kappan* [On-line]. Available on-line: http://pdkintl.org/kappan/kchi98 04.htm

Cloud, J. (2003, October 27). Inside the new SAT. *Time, 162* (17), 48–56.

Cochran-Smith, M, & Fries, M. K. (2001). Sticks, stones, and ideology: The discourse of reform in teacher education. *Educational Researcher, 30* (8), 3–15.

Codell, E. R. (1999). *Educating Esme: Diary of a teacher's first year.* Chapel Hill, NC: Algonquin Books.

Coles, G. (2000). *Misreading reading: The bad science that hurts children.* Portsmouth, NH: Heinemann.

———. (2003). The federal hickory stick for teaching reading. Retrieved February 26, 2003, from: http://www.educationnews.org/federal_hickory_stick_for_teachi .htm.

Conley, D. (2003). Mixed messages: What state high school tests communicate about student readiness for college. Eugene, OR: Center for Educational Policy

Research.

Daniels, H., & Zemelman, S. (2003/2004). Out with textbooks, in with learning. *Educational Leadership, 61* (4), 36–40.

Darling-Hammond, L. (2003, February 16). Standards and assessment: Where we are and what we need. *Teachers College Record.* Available on-line: http://www.tcre cord.org/PrintContent.asp?ContentID=11109.

Darling-Hammond, L. , & Youngs, P. (2002). Defining "highly qualified teachers": What does "scientifically-based research" actually tell us? *Educational Researcher, 31* (9), 13–25.

Davis, M. R. (2003, May 28). Ed. dept. invests $500,000 in team to tout its agenda. *Education Week, 22* (38), 1, 21.

Dempster, F. N. (1993, February). Exposing our students to less should help them learn more. *Phi Delta Kappan, 74* (6), 433–437.

Dewey, J. (1938). *Experience and education.* New York: Collier Books.

Dobbs, M. (2003, November 8). Education "miracle" has a math problem. *Washington Post.*

The effect of classroom practice on student achievement. (2003, May 27). *ResearchBrief, 1* (11). Retrieved May 29, 2003, from: http://www.ascd.org/publications/researchbrief/volume1/v1n11.html.

Egan, K. (2003). Testing what for what? *Educational Leadership, 61* (3), 27–30.

Eisner, E. W. (2003/2004). Preparing for today and tomorrow. *Educational Leadership, 61* (4), 6–10.

Elmore, R. F. (2003). A plea for strong practice. *Educational Leadership, 61* (3), 6–10.

Engel, M. (2000). *The struggle for control of public education: Market ideology vs. democratic values.* Philadelphia: Temple University Press.

ESEA/NCLB Analysis. (2003, February). Available on-line: http://www.ascd.org/cms/index.cfm?TheViewID=1634&ContentBordeDisplay=1&ptitle=ESEA%20An alysis%20-%20February%202003.

Fincher, C. (1990). *Trends in the predictive validity of the Scholastic Aptitude Test.* East Lansing, MI: National Center for Research on Teacher Learning. (ERIC Document Reproduction Service No. ED 395 968)

Fischer, K. (2003, March 6). Teen boycotts FCAT: "I'm not taking it." *St. Petersburg Times.*

Flinders, D. J., & Thornton, S. J., eds. (1997). *The curriculum studies reader.* New York: Routledge.

Franken, A. (2003). *Lies and the lying liars who tell them: A fair and balanced look at the Right.* New York: E. P. Dutton.

Freedman, S. W. (1995). Exam-based reform stifles student writing in the U.K. *Educational Leadership, 52* (6), 26–29.

Freire, P. (1993). *Pedagogy of the oppressed.* New York: Continuum.

Fullan, M. G. (1991). *The new meaning of educational change* (2nd ed.). New York: Teachers College Press.

Galehouse, M. (2003, February 3). Students opting out of tests: High stakes exams also draw parent protests. *The Arizona Republic.*

Gallagher, M. (2003a, July 25). Charter school's success challenges emphasis on certification. *Spartanburg Herald-Journal.*

———. (2003b, September 20). Science points clearly to how society is failing its young people. *Spartanburg Herald-Journal.*

Galley, M. (2003, December 9). Texas ponders easing route to secondary teaching. *Education Week, 23* (14), 16.

Gardner, H. (1999a). *The disciplined mind: What all students should understand.* New York: Simon and Schuster.

———. (1999b). *Intelligence reframed: Multiple intelligences for the 21st century.* New York: Basic Books.

———. (1996). *Leading minds: An anatomy of leadership.* New York: Basic Books.

———. (2002, September 4). The quality and qualities of educational research. *Education Week, 22* (1), 72, 49.

———. (1991). *The unschooled mind: How children think and how schools should teach.* New York: Basic Books.

Gehring, J. (2003, December 3). E.D. steers grants to pro-privatization groups, report charges. *Education Week, 23* (14), 22.

George, M. (2003, February 7). Poll: Policy at U-M unpopular. *Detroit Free Press.*

Gillespie, S. (2003, November 4). A battle over books in Texas. *Christian Science Monitor.*

Goodlad, J. I. (2003, April 23). A nation in wait. *Education Week, 22* (32), 36, 24, 25.

———. (2003/2004). Teaching what we hold sacred. *Educational Leadership, 61* (4), 18–21.

Goodnough, A. (2003, February 26). Schools chancellor stands by his choice of reading program. *New York Times.*

Gould, S. J. (1996). *The mismeasure of man.* Revised and expanded. New York: W. W. Norton and Company.

Hammond, B. (2003, November 24). Study: Test standards differ. *OregonLive.* Retrieved November 25, 2003, from: http://www.oregonlive.com.

Harmon, D. (2003, November 7). State approves biology text. *Austin American Statesman.*

Harvey, J. (2003). The matrix reloaded. *Educational Leadership, 61* (3), 18–21.

Harrell, R. W., Jr. (2003, October 7). State's PACT testing is about academic improvement. *The Greenville News.*

Harrison, S. (2003, December 9). Boycott of FCAT threatened. *Miami Herald.*

Henriques, D. B. (2003, September 2). Rising demands for testing push limits of its accuracy. *New York Times.*

Herbert, B. (2003, March 6). The war on schools. *The New York Times.*

Herszenhorn, D. M. (2004, January 7). For U.S. aid, city switches reading program. *New York Times.*

Hillocks, G., Jr. (2003). Fighting back: Assessing the assessments. *English Journal, 2* (4), 63–70.

———. (1995). *Teaching writing as reflective practice.* New York: Teachers College Press.

High school exit assessments: Features, effects, and costs. (2003). *Research brief, 1* (24). Available on-line: http://www.ascd.org/publications/researchbrief/volume1/v1n24.html.

Holton, G. (2003, April 25). An insider's view of "A Nation at Risk" and why it still matters. *Chronicle of Higher Education.* Retrieved April 28, 2003, from: http://chronicle.com/chronicle/v49/4933guide.htm.

Horvitz, L. (2003, May 9). Marketers cash in on reading. *Orlando Sentinel.*

Huse, S. M. (1993). *The collapse of evolution* (2nd ed.). Grand Rapids, MI: Baker Books.

Jenkins, N. J. (1992). *The Scholastic Aptitude Test as a predictor of academic success: A literature review*. East Lansing, MI: National Center for Research on Teacher Learning. (ERIC Document Reproduction Service No. ED 354 243)

Kauffman, D., Johnson, S. M., Kardos, S. M., Liu, E., & Peske, H. G. (2002, March). "Lost at sea": New teachers' experiences with curriculum and assessment. *Teachers College Record, 104* (2), 273–300.

Keller, B. (2003, November 12). Education school courses faulted as intellectually thin. *Education Week, 23*(11), 8. Retrieved December 1, 2003, from: http://www.edweek.org.

Kliebard, H. M. (1995). *The struggle for the American curriculum: 1893–1958*. New York: Routledge.

Kingsolver, B. (1990). *Animal dreams*. New York: Harper Perennial.

———. (1999). *The poisonwood bible*. New York: Harper Perennial.

———. (2002). *Small wonder*. New York: Perennial.

Kohn, A. (2000). *The case against standardized testing: Raising the scores, ruining the schools*. Portsmouth, NH: Heinemann.

Kralovec, E., & Buell, J. (2001). End homework now. *Educational Leadership, 58* (7), 39–42.

Krashen, S. (2002a, November 12). Exposing false claims about reading and reading instruction. Individual presentation at the NCTE national convention, Atlanta, GA.

———. (2003). False claims about phonemic awareness, phonics skills vs. whole language, and recreational reading. *NoChildLeft.Com, 1* (5). Available on-line: http://nochildleft.com/2003/may03reading.html

———. (2002b, June). Whole language and the great plummet of 1987–1992: An urban legend from California. *Phi Delta Kappan, 83* (10), 748–753.

Krauss, L. M., & Princehouse, P. (2003, November 24). Ohio faces a new challenge in intelligent-design debate. *Plain Dealer*.

Kristof, N. D. (2003, March 4). God, Satan and the media. *New York Times*.

Kronholz, J. (2003, December 25). School effort boosts business. *Charlotte Observer*.

Lagemann, E. C. (2000). *An elusive science: The troubling history of educational research*. Chicago: The University of Chicago Press.

Lambert, L, et al. (1995). *The constructivist leader*. New York: Teachers College Press.

Langland, C. (2003, May 29). Writer: Tests no help to learning. *Philadelphia Inquirer*.

Lemann, N. (1998, November) "Ready, read!" *Atlantic Monthly, 282* (5), 92–104.

Lemann, N. (2001, July 2). Testing limits: Can the president's education crusade survive beltway politics? *New Yorker*.

Lewis, A. C. (2002, November). A horse called NCLB. *Phi Delta Kappan, 84* (3), 179–180.

———. (2003, April). Students as commodities. *Phi Delta Kappan, 84* (8), 563–564.

Lofty, J. S. (2003). Standards and the politics of time and teacher professionalism. *English Education, 35* (3), 195–222.

Long, D. (2003, December 11). Report cards for K-4 being revamped. *Tennessean*.

Mabry, L. (1999, May). Writing to the rubric: Lingering effects of traditional standardized testing on direct writing assessment. *Phi Delta Kappan, 80* (9), 673–679.

Manzo, K. K. (2002, August 7). History repeats itself in Texas for textbook-review process. *Education Week, 21* (43), 11. Retrieved October 15, 2003, from: http://www.edweek.org/ew/ew_printstory.cfm?slug+43textbook.h21.

Manzo, K. K., & Hoff, D. J. (2003, February 5). Federal influence over curriculum exhibits growth. *Education Week, 22* (21), 1, 10–11.

Medina, J. (2003, May 13). Often, a bitter school choice: Almost as bad or far away. *New York Times*.

Miller, K. R. (1999). *Finding Darwin's God: A scientist's search for common ground between God and evolution*. New York: Perennial.

Mizell, H. (2003). Forum. *Journal of Staff Development, 24* (2), 80.

Molnar, A. (2003/2004). *Sixth Annual Report on Commercialism in Schools*: Cashing in on the classroom. *Educational Leadership, 61* (4) 79–84.

Moore, C., & O'Neill, P. (2002). *Practice in context: Situating the work of writing teachers*. Urbana, IL: National Council of Teachers of English.

Moore, S., & Simon, J. (2000). *It's getting better all the time: 100 greatest trends of the last 100 years*. Washington, DC: Cato Institute.

National Center for Educational Statistics. (2002). Writing 2002 major results. Retrieved July 10, 2003, from: http://nces.ed.gov/nationsreportcard/writing/results2002/.

National Commission on Writing in America's Schools and Colleges. (2003, April). The neglected "R": The need for a writing revolution. NY: The College Board. Available on-line: http://www.writingcommission.org/.

Neas, R. G. (2003, November 18). Funding a movement: U.S. Department of Education pours millions into groups advocating school vouchers and educational privatization. People for the American Way. Available on-line: http://www.pfaw.org.

Neill, M. (2003). The dangers of testing. *Educational Leadership, 60* (5), 43–46.

No victory in the voucher wars. (2003, December 30). *Plain Dealer*.

Ohanian, S. (2003, June). Capitalism, calculus, and conscience. *Phi Delta Kappan, 84* (10), 729–735.

Olson, L. (2003a, April 23). Quantity of coursework rises since 1983. *Education Week, 22* (32), 1, 14–17.

———. (2003b, March 5). Task force casts doubt on *Nation at Risk* accomplishments. *Education Week, 22* (25), 12.

Owens, R. G. (1995). *Organizational behavior in education* (5th ed.). Boston: Allyn and Bacon.

Paige, R. (2002). *Meeting the highly qualified teachers challenge: The Secretary's annual report on teacher quality*. Washington, DC: U.S. Department of Education.

Pardington, S. (2003, November 30). Montessori attitude tests well. *Contra Costa Times*.

Pinar, W. F., Reynolds, W. M., Slattery, P., & Taubman, P. M.. (1996). *Understanding curriculum: An introduction to the study of historical and contemporary curriculum discourse*. New York: Peter Lang.

Pinzur, M. I. (2003, December 9). Voucher schools mostly a blank slate. *Miami Herald*.

Popham, W. J. (2003). The seductive allure of data. *Educational Leadership, 60* (5), 48–51.

———. (2001a). Teaching to the test? *Educational Leadership, 58* (6), 16–20.

———. (2001b). *The Truth about testing: An educator's call to action*. Alexandria, VA: Association for Supervision and Curriculum Development.

———. (1999). Why standardized tests don't measure educational quality. *Educational Leadership, 56* (6), 8–15.

Raymo, C. (1998). *Skeptics and true believers: The exhilarating connection between science and religion.* New York: MJF Books.

Research-based characteristics of high-quality teacher preparation. (2003, February 19). *Research brief, 1* (4). Available on-line: http://www.ascd.org/publications/researchbrief/volume1/v1n4.html.

Rich, A. (2001). *Arts of the possible: Essays and conversations.* New York: W. W. Norton and Co.

Rimer, S. (2003, March 3). Quest to be No. 1 can undermine education. *Spartanburg Herald-Journal.*

Ringer, R. J., & Bineham, J. L. (1995, November 10). Education and the market metaphor. *University Chronicle.* Available on-line: http://web.stcloudstate.edu/bineham/editorials88-00/education_and_the_market_metapho.htm.

Rogers, C. (1995). *On becoming a person: a therapist's view of psychotherapy.* New York: Mariner Books.

Routman, R. (1996). *Literacy at the crossroads: Crucial talk about reading, writing, and other writing dilemmas.* Portsmouth, NH: Heinemann.

———. (2003). *Reading essentials: The specifics you need to teach reading well.* Portsmouth, NH: Heinemann.

Schemo, D. J., & Fessenden, F. (2003, December 3). Gains in Houston schools: How real are they? *New York Times.*

Schmoker, M. (2003, February 12). Planning for failure? *Education Week, 22* (22), 39. Retrieved February 12, 2003, from: http://www.edweek.org.

Shafersman, S. (2003, July 9). Texas textbook adoption: An historical analysis. Texas Citizens for Science. Retrieved October 15, 2003, from: http://www.txscience.org.

Silverman, D. (1993). *Interpreting qualitative data: Methods for analyzing talk, text, and interaction.* Thousand Oaks, CA: Sage Publications.

Silverman, J. (2003, November 23). Law is frustrating for special ed. *Seattle Times.*

Sizer, T. R. (2003, April 23). Two reports. *Education Week, 22* (32), 36, 24, 25.

Slavin, R. E. (2003). A reader's guide to scientifically based research. *Educational Leadership, 60* (5), 12–16.

Smith, M. B. (1949). *And madly teach: A layman looks at public school education.* Chicago: Henry Regnery.

Strauss, V. (2003, February 4). Grades may not be measuring up. *Washington Post.*

Texas students, teachers get cash for passing exams. (2003, December 15). *Houston Chronicle.*

Textbook adoption needs second look: Process not serving children. (2001, May 21). The Center for Education Reform. Retrieved October 15, 2003, from: http://edreform.com/press/2001/textbook.htm.

The textbook conundrum: What are the children learning and who decides? (2001, May). The Center for Education Reform. Retrieved October 15, 2003, from: http://edreform.com/press/2001/textbook.htm.

Thomas, P. L. (1999). A new honesty in education—Positivist measures in a post-modern world. *Contemporary Education, 71* (1), 51–55.

Thomas, P. (2001). *Lou LaBrant—A woman's life, a teacher's life.* Huntington, NY: Nova Science Publishers, Inc.

Thomas, P. (2003, October 21). Politicians should stay out of the business of running schools. *The Greenville News.*

Thoreau, H. D. (1962). Civil disobedience. In J. W. Krutch (Ed.), *Walden and other writings by Henry David Thoreau* (pp. 85–104). New York: Bantam Books.

Torres, M. (2003, February 1). Student rebels at taking standardized test. *San Antonio Express-News*.

Vonnegut, K. (1980). *Player piano*. New York: Delta.

Warner, A. L. (1993). If the shoe no longer fits, wear it anyway? *English Journal, 82* (5), 76–80.

Watras, J. (2004). *Philosophic conflicts in American education, 1893–2000*. New York: Pearson/Allyn and Bacon.

Watson, A. (1998, June). The newspaper's responsibility. *Phi Delta Kappan, 79* (10), 728–734.

Weaver, C. (1996). *Teaching grammar in context*. Portsmouth, NH: Heinemann.

Wilhelm, J. D., Baker, T. N., & Dube, J. (2001). *Strategic reading: Guiding students to lifelong literacy, 6–12*. Portsmouth, NH: Heinemann.

Williams, J. M. (1990). *Style: Toward clarity and grace*. Chicago: The University of Chicago Press.

Williams, T. (1985). *The glass menagerie*. In S. Barnet, M. Berman, & W. Burto (Eds.), *An introduction to literature: Fiction, poetry, drama* (pp. 967–1025). Boston: Little, Brown and Company.

Williams, W. (2003, October 26). The key to education? No excuses. *Spartanburg Herald-Journal*.

Winerip, M. (2003, April 30). Discovering crisis, again and again. *New York Times*.

Wiske, M. S. (1998). *Teaching for understanding: Linking research with practice*. San Francisco: Jossey-Bass.

Yatvin, J. (2002). Babes in the woods: The wanderings of the National Reading Panel. *Phi Delta Kappan, 83* (5), 364–369.

———. (2003, April 30). I told you so! The misrepresentation and misuse of The National Reading Panel report. *Education Week, 22* (33), 56, 44, 45.

Zemelman, S., H. Daniels, & A. Hyde. (1998). *Best practice: New standards for teaching and learning in America's schools* (2nd ed.). Portsmouth, NH: Heinemann.

Zimmermann, J., & C. Brown. (2003, April). Let them eat more phonics. *Phi Delta Kappan, 84* (8), 603–605.